Es

Singapore

by

CHRISTOPHER NAYLOR

Christopher Naylor is a travel writer specialising in Southeast Asia where he worked for several years as a journalist and public relations consultant.

AA

Produced by AA Publishing

Written by Christopher Naylor
Verified by Nick Hanna
Peace and Quiet section
by Paul Sterry
Original photography
by Paul Kenward

Revised third edition 1996
Reprinted (three times) 1995
Revised second edition 1994
First published 1992

Edited, designed and produced by AA Publishing.

Distributed in the United Kingdom by AA Publishing, Norfolk House, Priestley Road, Basingstoke, Hampshire, RG24 9NY.

A CIP catalogue record for this book is available from the British Library.

ISBN 0 7495 1323 3

Published by AA Publishing, a trading name of Automobile Association Developments Limited, whose registered office is Norfolk House, Priestley Road, Basingstoke, Hampshire, RG24 9NY.
Registered number 1878835.

Colour separation: Mullis Morgan Ltd, London.

Printed by: Printers S.R.L., Trento, Italy

Front cover picture: *Chinese dragon*

Contents

INTRODUCTION 4

BACKGROUND 7

WHAT TO SEE 17

PEACE AND QUIET
Wildlife and Countryside in Singapore 49

FOOD AND DRINK 55

SHOPPING 69

ACCOMMODATION 77

CULTURE, ENTERTAINMENT, NIGHTLIFE 85

WEATHER AND WHEN TO GO 91

HOW TO BE A LOCAL 92

CHILDREN 96

TIGHT BUDGET 97

SPECIAL EVENTS 98

SPORT 104

DIRECTORY 107

LANGUAGE 125

INDEX 126

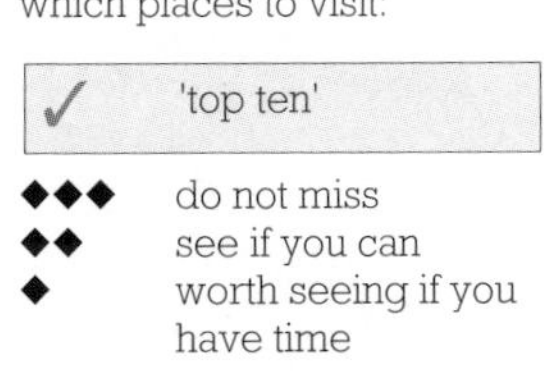
This book employs a simple rating system to help choose which places to visit:

✓ 'top ten'

◆◆◆ do not miss
◆◆ see if you can
◆ worth seeing if you have time

Maps and Plans

Locator 4
Singapore 14–15
Singapore City 18–19
Chinatown 24
Colonial Singapore and Fort Canning 28–9
Islands 35
Sentosa 44
Orchard Road – Shopping 74
MRT (metro) 120

Country Distinguishing Signs
On the maps, international distinguishing signs have been used to indicate those countries which surround Singapore.
Thus:

(RI) = Indonesia (MAL) = Malaysia

INTRODUCTION

Singapore is an island of paradoxes. With no natural resources and no agriculture, it has become the richest nation in Asia after Japan and oil-rich Brunei, thanks to the hard work and resourcefulness of its 2.9 million population. It is an industrial state and yet maintains enviable standards of pollution control and greenness; one of Lee Kuan Yew's best decisions during his 31-year premiership was to turn Singapore into a 'Garden of the Orient', with the result that strikingly coloured tropical flowers, statuesque trees, luscious ferns and rampant vines greet the eye wherever you look, softening the outlines of road verges, bridges and housing blocks, and disguising the fact that Singapore is now one almost unbroken conurbation. Perhaps the biggest paradox of all is the fact that Singapore receives some 7 million visitors a year and yet it has few of the compelling attractions – such as palm-fringed beaches or wild nightlife – of its neighbours. Singapore does not even have the appeal of the strange

The skyscrapers of the Central Business District punctuate the city's skyline, with the Singapore River curving around the heart of old, colonial Singapore a stone's throw away

and the exotic – everyone speaks English, the high-tech tower blocks are the same as in any other city, and the goods in the shops come from all over the world.

So why do so many people come here? The simple answer is for a first-class tourist infrastructure which ensures that, whilst they are enjoying what Singapore has to offer, visitors are made to feel utterly pampered. Hotels and restaurants are excellent, service is friendly, taxis are cheap, guided tours are well planned and inexpensive, and the island's glittering shopping malls are packed with consumer goods in greater variety than you can find almost anywhere else in the world.

In past decades the Government has been criticised for neglecting its historic buildings and bulldozing turn-of-the-century shop-houses to make way for an avalanche of concrete and steel. That policy has long since changed, and after a successful pilot project to restore Emerald Hill (off Orchard Road), all the main ethnic districts (including Chinatown, Little India and Arab Street) have been subject to huge restoration programmes. Nowhere else in Asia, it could be argued, has devoted so much attention to preserving its architectural heritage in this way – even if the end result has been to turn enclaves of the city into the equivalent of cultural theme parks. Indigenous arts, crafts and culture are also being given greater encouragement with the establishment of a new Arts Museum, new theatre and performance venues, and other initiatives; plans are also

afoot to encourage more international arts and entertainment events to the city to attract overseas travellers.

It is fashionable amongst old Asia hands to deride Singapore, by contrast with its neighbours, as dull, antiseptic and over-regimented. Visitors, on the other hand, visibly relax on arrival, and welcome the island's orderliness, its cleanliness, lack of crime and litter, its parks and greenery – all a welcome contrast to polluted and frenetic Bangkok or the pressure-cooker atmosphere of Hong Kong. Even so, the Singapore Tourist Promotion Board is well aware that cleanliness and comfort do not of themselves attract visitors for long, or bring them back. Great hopes are pinned on the joint Indonesian/Singaporean venture to develop the island of Bintan, which lies to the south of Singapore, and turn it into a resort island with marinas and water sports facilities. The latest marketing drive is to create more 'city and resort' packages such as this, taking advantage of the excellent range of regional flights to make Singapore the launch pad for forays further afield in the Far East. The aim is to change the perception of Singapore as one huge shopping arcade with restaurants attached, and the plan will no doubt succeed. You do not have to wait until it does, however, to enjoy Singapore, especially if you get out of the downtown area. The island's parks, gardens and nature reserves are little visited, except at weekends, and provide a rare chance to study tropical flora and fauna close up and in relative comfort. A trip around the harbour, where ships from every corner of the globe are unloaded day and night, will give you an insight into the workings of a modern port, the busiest in the world, and with the help of Joseph Conrad's novels and a little imagination you can easily envisage what this bazaar of the Orient might have been like in the days of sailing ships and steam. Tours of colonial Singapore, Chinatown and Little India will give you further insights into Singapore's historical roots and lead you to ponder the remarkable fact that so many different races and ethnic groups live together in harmony and proudly proclaim their Singaporean identity, whilst retaining their diverse cultural traditions.

BACKGROUND

'Sir Stamford Raffles landed here on the 28th January 1819 and, with genius and perception, changed the destiny of Singapore from an obscure fishing village to a great seaport and modern metropolis.'

This inscription on the pedestal of the statue of Sir Stamford Raffles, which stands by Parliament House on the bank of the Singapore River, sums up one half of the history of Singapore. In due course, perhaps, there will be a second statue, this time, of Lee Kuan Yew, with an inscription to the effect that he, with shrewdness and steadfast purpose, guided Singapore as Prime Minister for 31 years and turned this tiny island state into a proud and prosperous Asian nation. Singapore has been shaped by these two

Merlion Park is home to the half-fish, half-lion Merlion, created to symbolise Singapore – the 'Lion City' – and her maritime status

Restored colonial grandeur – Raffles Hotel remains the 'Grand Old Lady of the East'

towering figures and the policies which both pursued have much in common. Both embraced the concept of Singapore as a multi-ethnic state. The main difference is that Raffles believed in the segregation of the races as a means to harmony, whereas Government policy under Lee Kuan Yew had deliberately sought to break up racial ghettos, by creating mixed housing estates – and, through education and propaganda, the Government has persuaded the people of this island that they are first and foremost Singaporean, no matter what their racial or religious background.

It has not been difficult for a single individual to dominate Singapore. After all, it is a tiny island: some 224 square miles (580sq km) in area, roughly diamond-shaped and located some 85 miles (136km) north of the equator, just off the southern tip of peninsular Malaysia. The location is all important. Singapore stands at the maritime crossroads of Southeast Asia, at the

point where all ships must pass, whether they are heading northwards up to Hong Kong, China, Taiwan or Japan, south and east to Indonesia and Australasia, or westwards to India, Arabia and Europe.

Raffles was a talented and energetic servant of the British East India Company who recognised Singapore's strategic position before anyone else did. At the age of 30, when he was already Lieutenant General of Java and a fluent Malay speaker, he sought permission from Lord Hastings, Governor General of India and in charge of British operations in the East, to establish a colony on Singapore. Raffles regarded the island as the best base from which to compete with the Dutch, already established at Malacca on the Malay peninsula, for control of Southeast Asian trade and he recognised the potential of Singapore as a port and trading post.

Establishing a new British colony for once involved no violence and bloodshed. When Raffles landed in 1819 the island had a population of some two or three hundred people and was controlled by the Sultan of Johor, the southernmost sultanate of the Malay peninsula. Raffles signed a treaty, paid a small sum of money and left William Farquhar in charge of clearing the jungle and mangrove swamps so that houses and warehouses could be built.

The new colonial trading post acted as a magnet to itinerant traders from China, Malaysia and Indonesia, 'sea gypsies' who made a meagre living buying goods here and selling them wherever they could. Arriving in Singapore, they either lived on their boats or built ramshackle villages wherever they could clear a patch of jungle. Returning to Singapore three years later, Raffles is said not to have been pleased by the chaos and lack of order that he found. He personally drew up a development plan for Singapore, allocating separate areas of the island to different racial groups following the principle that was then regarded as the best way of avoiding racial tension – segregation. Raffles left Singapore a year later – in 1823 – and died in 1826, at the young age of 42, of a brain tumour. Despite his short sojourn in Singapore, his plan for the island left an indelible mark, and the legacy can still be seen today in the survival

Training singing birds is a popular hobby which culminates in regular concerts, where trainers compare notes

of the Chinatown, Arab Street and Little India communities, not to mention the division of the land either side of the Singapore River into a northern administrative district and a southern commercial quarter.

Over the next 40 years, Singapore developed an infrastructure, using Indian convict labour to clear the jungle and lay down roads and services. The port boomed and Chinese indentured labourers were brought to Singapore by the shipload to work as porters in the *godowns*, or warehouses, loading and unloading precious cargoes of tea and silk, ebony and ivory, spices and textiles – not to mention the Indian opium which less-than-scrupulous British merchants traded with the Chinese for commodities that were in demand back home.

The opening of the Suez Canal in 1869 gave a further boost to Singapore as more and more steam-powered ships made the journey between Europe and Asia, using Singapore as a base for refuelling. The demand for Malaysian tin, and then the rapid growth of the regional rubber industry – encouraged by HN Ridley, Director of Singapore's Botanical Gardens – further added to the range of cargoes passing through Singapore. As a result, Singapore entered the 20th century as the seventh busiest port in the world, and a flavour of life at this time is captured in several of Joseph Conrad's stories; *Lord Jim*, *The End of the Tether* and *The Rescue* are all based on Conrad's experiences as a merchant seaman making regular visits to Singapore between 1886 and 1894.

Another regular visitor was Somerset Maugham. Between the two World Wars he regularly observed expatriate behaviour from the comfort of the Raffles Hotel, the centre of European social life and a rich mine of material for his poignant short stories. He describes the English 'in their topees and white ducks, speeding past in motor cars or at leisure in their rickshaws wearing a nonchalant air. The rulers of these teeming peoples take their authority with a smiling unconcern.' That complacency was about to be shattered, however. As early as 1921 work had begun to strengthen Singapore's seaward defences and prepare the island to serve as a base for the Royal Navy. Hostilities between Japan and China broke out in 1927 and by the beginning of World War II it was clear that Japan was intent on controlling all of Asia. Singapore was taken on 15 February 1942. The British had expected an invasion from the sea and had prepared the southern defences accordingly. The Japanese won an easy victory by invading from Malaya, to the unprotected north. Winston Churchill called it 'the largest capitulation in British history'. The Japanese were themselves to capitulate to the Allies on 21 August 1945, but in the intervening three years the Chinese population was treated with especial brutality and many British prisoners died in the disease-ridden prison camps or working as forced labour on schemes such as the infamous Burma railroad.

The British were welcomed back at Liberation, but the political climate had changed here, as it had all over the Empire. Singaporeans had had enough of being ordered about, whether by the Japanese or by more benign colonial masters. The desire for independence was shared equally by the people of Malaya and Singapore, but the issue was clouded by internal power struggles and the activities of the Communist Party of Malaya, which believed that the only way to wrest independence was by the force of arms. The 12 years, from 1948 to 1960, during which British forces fought Communist guerrillas in the Malay jungle, held up what might otherwise have been a swifter transfer of power. In the event, a new constitution granting self-government to Singapore, was not approved by the British Parliament until 1959.

One member of the Singaporean delegation that hammered out the details of the new constitution in London was Lee Kuan Yew, a young Cambridge-educated lawyer who founded the People's Action Party in 1954. The terms of the 1959 Constitution made provision for an elected Assembly of 51 members. The PAP won 43 of the 51 seats, with some 53 per cent of the votes cast, and Lee Kuan Yew was formally appointed Singapore's first Prime Minister in June 1959 – a position he was to hold for the next 31 years, until his retirement in the autumn of 1990. Ironically, Lee Kuan Yew and the PAP were regarded as dangerously left-wing by the doom mongers of the Empire, who predicted a sorry future for Singapore under his control. It would perhaps be more accurate to describe the original PAP as a 'broad church', embracing both Communists and conservatives. Such unlikely bedfellows could not but fall out before long and, in the years leading up to full independence in 1963, some of the more radical members broke away to form opposition parties.

Lee Kuan Yew's strategy for remaining in power was based on the assumption that the left-wing threat would disappear once Singaporeans tasted affluence. To that end, he led Singapore into a merger with the Federation of Malaysia, arguing that Singapore needed raw materials, which the island lacked, on favourable terms and could only prosper with a wider market for its goods than Singapore alone could provide. Malaysia, however, turned out to be a somewhat reluctant partner, resistant to the idea of a 'common market' and antagonistic to the idea of the PAP playing a wider role in the affairs of the Malaysian Federation. On 9 August 1965, less than two years after leading Singapore into the Federation, Lee Kuan Yew signed the severance declaration. Singapore was now fully independent – and entirely alone.

Economic analysts argue endlessly over the underlying reasons for the astonishing growth that Singapore then experienced under Lee Kuan Yew's guidance. The Chinese work ethic, the desire to achieve, respect for authority; legislation limiting the power of trade unions and putting a ceiling on wages to ensure that the cost of labour remained cheap; the absence of controls on outside investment, and of import and export duties – all of these contributed in some measure to an astonishing achievement. Between 1968 and 1985, Singapore achieved average economic growth of 9 per cent per annum, one of the highest rates of growth the world has ever seen. At the heart of Lee Kuan Yew's strategy was the determination to base Singapore's economy on manufacturing, rather than on service sector activities like banking, tourism and entrepôt trade. These activities soon followed and, today, make a substantial contribution to the economy, but Lee Kuan

Looking resolutely towards the future, Singapore still values its traditions and colourful Chinese opera is just one of the many cultural and artistic events to be experienced

Yew's goals of full employment, decent and affordable housing for everyone, high standards of education and health care, and an efficient transport infrastructure have all been paid for essentially from the strong performance of the industrial sector. Singapore, Lee Kuan Yew and the PAP have their critics, of course. Western commentators who regard the regime as illiberal point to the fact that some left-wing politicians are still languishing in prison, to which they were condemned without trial in the 1960s, for 'creating tension and unrest in the state'. Lee hit the headlines in the 1980s for espousing what the western media presented as neo-Nazi views on selective breeding, encouraging Singaporean graduates not to marry 'less intelligent' spouses as this would endanger Singapore's genetic stock. Some newspapers and magazines are not available in Singapore because they have been critical of Government policy. Singaporeans are subject to numerous laws and propaganda campaigns – against smoking, spitting, littering; against speaking Chinese dialects (Mandarin is preferred) and even against roller-skating and chewing gum in public places.

You will not, however, find many Singaporeans who complain against this alleged authoritarianism. They can see the point – and the beneficial effects – of many laws and are quite capable of laughing at the odd excesses, like the 'love boat' scheme organised by the Social Development Unit designed to bring unmarried graduates together for match-making disco cruises and beach parties. Singaporeans, by and large, are quite content with their lot, and the post-war generation, articulate, well educated and prosperous, see

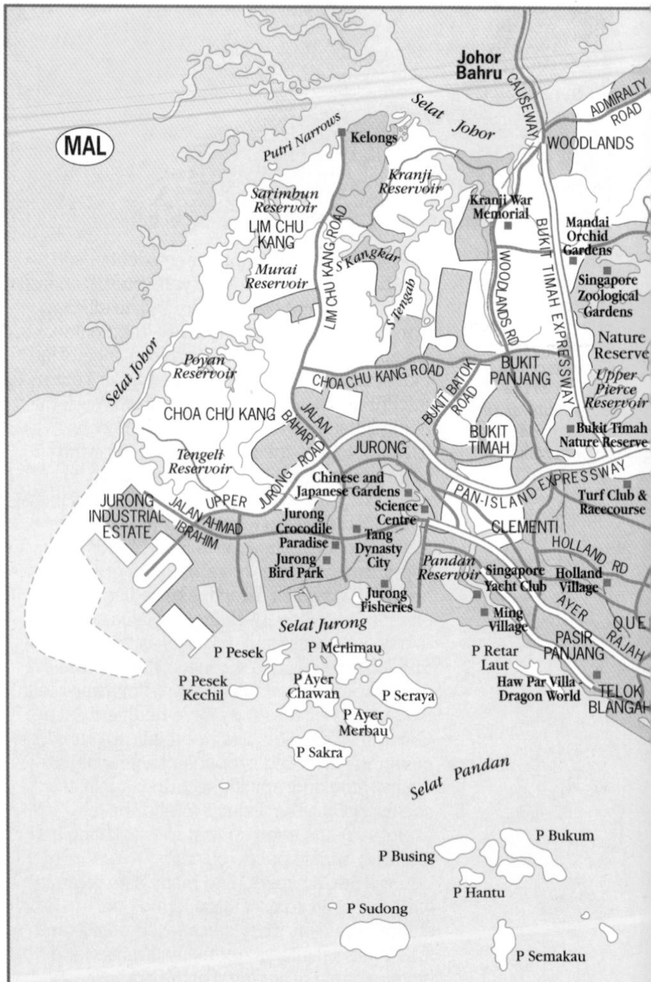

themselves as the fortunate heirs to a society relatively untroubled by the evils of corruption, drugs, violence, vandalism and crime. They are not complacent, however. The Porsche- or Mercedes-driving Singaporean yuppie, sporting filofax, mobile phone, Rolex and designer label clothes, is a figure to be mocked in local

newspaper cartoons, but he or she is far from being a fictional creation; more thoughtful Singaporeans are concerned that material prosperity has been achieved at the expense of the soul. Singapore does not have many writers, artists or designers. It does not even have an indigenous pop music industry – local singers do cover versions of hits from Hong Kong or Taiwan. Under the new Prime Minister, Goh Chok Tong, Singapore has set itself a new goal for the next 25 years: to become a society that adds value through creativity and brainpower. Whether creativity can thrive in a highly regulated society remains to be seen. Japan has achieved it and is regarded as leading Asia in matters of style, design, commercial art, advertising and fashion. If Singapore has its way Japan will soon find itself with a formidable rival.

Siong Lim Temple recalls Beijing's Forbidden City. It is one of numerous Chinese temples on the island, where the age-old rituals are still performed – even if the worshippers are more likely to be wearing buisiness suits than traditional costumes

WHAT TO SEE

Singapore is a small island, some 224 square miles (580sq km) in area and roughly diamond shaped. The Singapore River still forms the island's focal point. It was here that Sir Stamford Raffles landed in 1819 to claim the island for the British and from here that settlement spread inland. Today the river divides the downtown area in two. To the north lies the hotel and shopping district. Here, too, you will find some of the oldest colonial buildings: Parliament House, the courts, City Hall and the Victoria Theatre, all standing in a compact group around the Padang, a great swathe of level grass used as a parade ground and venue for cricket and rugby. This area is linked to the southern bank and the financial district of Singapore, with its gleaming skyscrapers, by a series of bridges, some dating from the colonial era. Chinatown also lies to the south, along with Clifford Pier, the departure point for harbour and river cruises.
The downtown area encompasses most of the sights that are of interest to tourists and it is easy to get about by taxi, bus or MRT (Mass Rapid Transit system – see **Public Transport** in **Directory** section). Further afield, to the west of the island, lies Jurong, an expanding manufacturing district but also the centre of a number of attractions, including the Chinese and Japanese Gardens, the Bird Park and the Science Centre.
The southern tip of the Malaysian peninsula is separated from Singapore by the narrow Johor Straits and the two are linked by a causeway; it takes about 30 minutes to reach the Malaysian town of Johor Bahru on the northern bank of the Straits and it is easy enough to make the trip, either by taxi or limousine or by joining a tour. You can also take day trips to the Indonesian Islands of Batam and Bintan. Both islands are undergoing joint development by the Singaporean and Indonesian Governments – Batam as an economic development zone (although with considerable emphasis on tourism) and Bintan as a resort centre. They are popular with Singaporeans for weekend breaks and well known for their beaches and delicious seafood.

◆

ARAB STREET

Commercial success has changed Arab Street. What was once a characterful road lined with individual shops selling sundry goods to the local Muslim community is now more geared towards yen- and dollar-wielding tourists. For old times' sake you can haggle over the price of brightly-coloured fabrics or a woven basket, but the shop-keeper will probably display a take-it-or-leave-it attitude.
If you are interested in Singapore's history, explore the lanes on either side of Arab Street, where names like Baghdad, Sultan, Muscat and Jeddah Street remind us that this was once the heartland of Singapore's Muslim community. Muslim traders from Malaya, Indonesia, India and even some

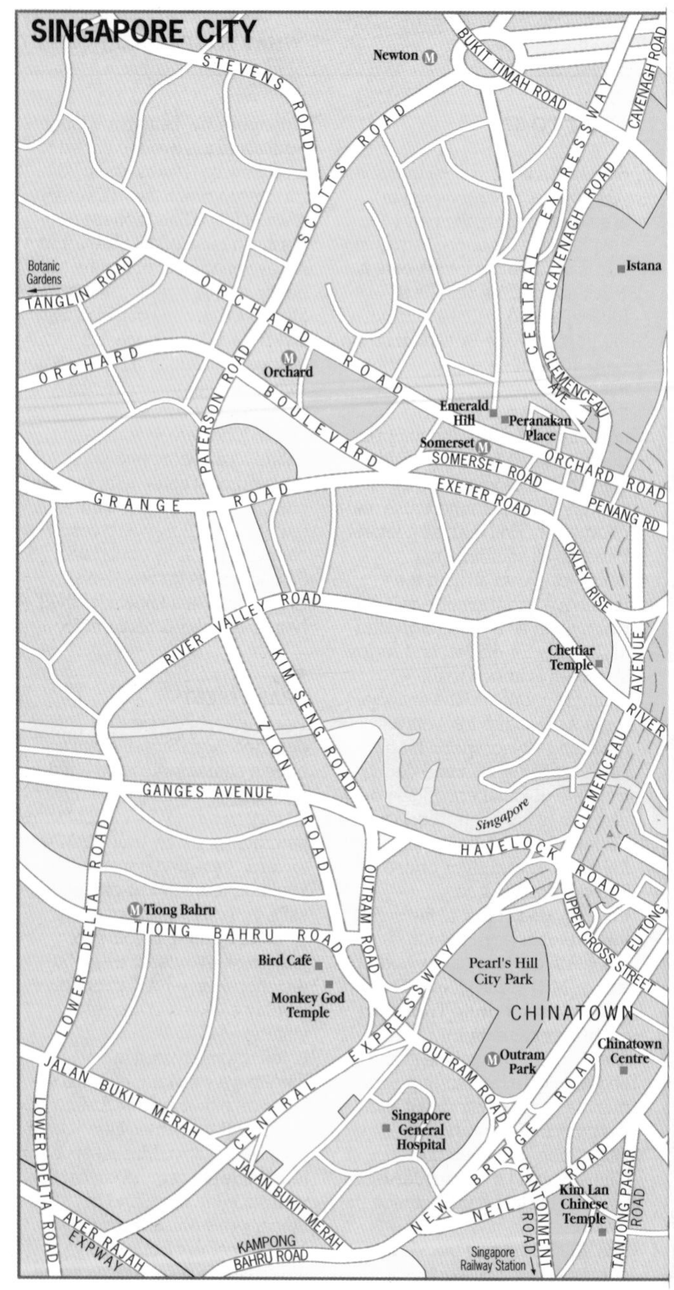
SINGAPORE CITY
Newton
Stevens Road
Bukit Timah Road
Central Expressway
Cavenagh Road
Scotts Road
Istana
Botanic Gardens
Tanglin Road
Orchard Road
Orchard
Paterson Road
Orchard Boulevard
Emerald Hill
Peranakan Place
Somerset
Somerset Road
Clemenceau Ave
Grange Road
Exeter Road
Penang Rd
Oxley Rise
River Valley Road
Chettiar Temple
River Valley Road
Kim Seng Road
Zion Road
Ganges Avenue
Singapore
Havelock Road
Clemenceau Avenue
Outram Road
Lower Delta Road
Tiong Bahru
Tiong Bahru Road
Upper Cross Street
Eu Tong Sen Street
Bird Café
Monkey God Temple
Pearl's Hill City Park
CHINATOWN
Central Expressway
Outram Park
Chinatown Centre
Jalan Bukit Merah
Lower Delta Road
Outram Road
New Bridge Road
Singapore General Hospital
Neil Road
Cantonment Road
Kim Lan Chinese Temple
Tanjong Pagar Road
Ayer Rajah Expway
Kampong Bahru Road
Singapore Railway Station

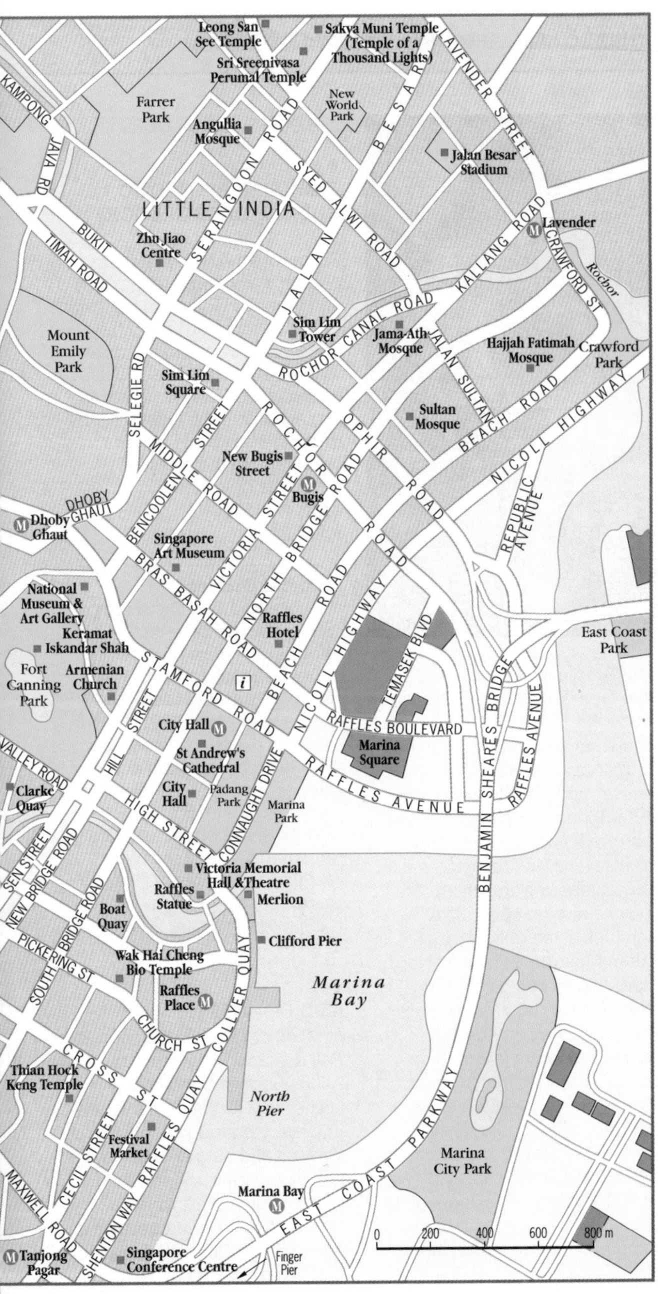
Leong San See Temple
Sakya Muni Temple (Temple of a Thousand Lights)
Sri Sreenivasa Perumal Temple
Farrer Park
New World Park
Angullia Mosque
Jalan Besar Stadium
LITTLE INDIA
Zhu Jiao Centre
Lavender
Rochor
Mount Emily Park
Sim Lim Tower
Jama-Ath Mosque
Hajjah Fatimah Mosque
Crawford Park
Sim Lim Square
Sultan Mosque
New Bugis Street
Bugis
Dhoby Ghaut
Singapore Art Museum
National Museum & Art Gallery
Keramat Iskandar Shah
Raffles Hotel
East Coast Park
Fort Canning Park
Armenian Church
City Hall
St Andrew's Cathedral
Marina Square
Clarke Quay
City Hall
Padang Park
Marina Park
Victoria Memorial Hall &Theatre
Raffles Statue
Merlion
Boat Quay
Clifford Pier
Wak Hai Cheng Bio Temple
Raffles Place
Marina Bay
Thian Hock Keng Temple
North Pier
Festival Market
Marina City Park
Marina Bay
Tanjong Pagar
Singapore Conference Centre
Finger Pier
0 200 400 600 800 m
KAMPONG
JAVA RD
BUKIT TIMAH ROAD
SERANGOON ROAD
SYED ALWI ROAD
JALAN BESAR
LAVENDER STREET
KALLANG ROAD
CRAWFORD ST
ROCHOR CANAL ROAD
JALAN SULTAN
BEACH ROAD
NICOLL HIGHWAY
SELEGIE RD
MIDDLE ROAD
ROCHOR ROAD
OPHIR ROAD
REPUBLIC AVENUE
DHOBY GHAUT
BENCOOLEN STREET
VICTORIA STREET
NORTH BRIDGE ROAD
BRAS BASAH ROAD
TEMASEK BLVD
STAMFORD ROAD
RAFFLES BOULEVARD
BENJAMIN SHEARES BRIDGE
RAFFLES AVENUE
HILL STREET
CONNAUGHT DRIVE
VALLEY ROAD
HIGH STREET
SEN STREET
NEW BRIDGE ROAD
SOUTH BRIDGE ROAD
PICKERING ST
COLLYER QUAY
CHURCH ST
CROSS ST
CECIL STREET
RAFFLES QUAY
SHENTON WAY
MAXWELL ROAD
EAST COAST PARKWAY

Bird Concert's dawn chorus

from Arabia, were moved here from their original settlements by the Singapore River because Sir Stamford Raffles wanted their land for his own purposes. The area around Arab Street, known as Kampong Glam, was a former mangrove swamp, and today's streets were laid out using Indian convict labour from the 1820s. Today's Muslim community worships at the gold-domed **Sultan Mosque**, in nearby North Bridge Road, rebuilt in 1928 (open outside times of prayer). On Beach Road, the **Hajjah Fatimah Mosque** is a more delicate building, dating from 1846 and the oldest surviving mosque in Singapore. Hajjah Fatimah paid for its construction with the wealth she amassed as an entrepreneur, making a great success of her late husband's shipping and trading business.
MRT: Bugis

ARMENIAN APOSTOLIC CHURCH OF ST GREGORY

Hill Street

Singapore's oldest surviving church was completed in 1835 and George Coleman, architect of Parliament House and the Supreme Court originally gave it a dome reflecting the circular shape of the interior. This was replaced with the existing spire in 1850, a structure that sits oddly above the classical porticoes below.
MRT: City Hall
Bus: 124

National Orchids

The graveyard of the Church of St Gregory contains the weathered tombs of early Armenian settlers – refugees from Turkey – including that of Agnes Joaquim. In 1893, Miss Joaquim discovered a striking purple orchid growing in her garden. Henry Ridley, Director of the Singapore Botanic Gardens, named the hitherto unknown hybrid *Vanda Miss Joaquim* in her honour. That orchid has now become Singapore's national flower.

◆

BIRD CONCERT

Junction of Tiong Bahru and Seng Poh Roads

At 08.00hrs on Sunday, this corner café is the venue for an unusual gathering of songbirds. They sit and sing in their ornate bamboo cages, suspended on poles, while their owners sit, listening, comparing notes and discussing training techniques.
MRT: Outram Park or Tiong Bahru

◆◆◆
BOTANIC GARDENS ✓

Main entrance: Cluny Road, junction with Holland Road
This 128-acre (52ha) garden lies only minutes away from the bustle of Orchard Road. It is an ideal hideaway for a quiet walk (during the week) and a must for anyone with an interest in tropical flora. Trail leaflets point out some of the more spectacular specimens and economically important plants. Without the Botanic Gardens, Singapore would not be the Garden City that it is. Botanists working here have introduced and propagated many of the trees and shrubs that make the island so colourful. In this they are continuing a tradition established by Sir Stamford Raffles who set up Singapore's first botanic garden in 1822 with the aim of introducing new food and spice plants to the island. The Botanic Gardens are beautifully landscaped, with areas of primary forest giving way to lakes and specialist rose, marsh and fern gardens. The recently opened **National Orchid Garden** displays over 50,000 orchids and other tropical species tiered between fountains and water features. Other new attractions include a **Spice Garden** and the prosaically-titled **Economic Garden** featuring medicinal plants.
Open: daily, 05.00hrs–midnight.
Bus: 7, 105, 106, 123 or 174

'Mad Ridley'
The present Botanic Gardens date back to 1859 and one of its early directors was Henry Ridley, who introduced rubber trees to Southeast Asia. The first seeds of this Brazilian tree were sent from London's Kew Gardens and propagated here in 1877. Ridley's zealous campaign to persuade local landowners to develop rubber plantations earned him the nickname 'Mad Ridley', but his efforts paid off: rubber production remains a staple of the regional economy.

◆
BUKIT TIMAH NATURE RESERVE

Upper Bukit Timah Road (entrance from Hindhede Drive), 7½ miles (12km) from Orchard Road
Bukit Timah is Singapore's highest hill (533 feet/162m) and the summit is surrounded by 200 acres (81ha) of primary jungle. Well-marked pathways thread beneath the towering forest canopy and there is also a new 2-mile (3.5km) mountain biking trail. If you are quiet and observant you may catch sight of tropical snakes and pangolin

The attraction of the National Orchid Garden

(anteaters). Squirrels are less shy and the long-tailed macaque monkeys have little fear of humans. Large and colourful butterflies feed on the vegetation, which includes numerous tropical ferns, climbers and even some carnivorous, pitcher-shaped Monkey Cups.
Open: 08.30–18.00hrs (tel: 470 9900).
MRT: Newton, then SBS bus 67, 170, 171, 182

◆

CHANGI PRISON CHAPEL AND MUSEUM

Changi Prison, Changi Village
Changi Village is located on the northeastern tip of the island, north of Changi airport. The chapel is a replica of the simple structure built by prisoners of war while Singapore was under Japanese occupation. The museum contains mementoes of prison life, including materials from the Thai–Burma railway where many POWs died.
Open: Monday to Saturday 09.30–16.30hrs.
Closed: Sunday and public holidays.
MRT: Tanah Merah then bus 2
Bus: 2, 14

◆

CHETTIAR TEMPLE

Tank Road
The original temple, completed in 1860 and dedicated to the Hindu deity Subramaniam, was entirely rebuilt in 1984. The entrance *gopuram*, or gateway, leads into a covered courtyard with a ceiling carved with lotus flowers. Glass panels engraved with numerous deities are positioned so that they are illuminated by the rising and setting sun.

The Chettiars
The Chettiars came from the Madras area of southern India and were encouraged to settle in Singapore by the British, where they followed their traditional trade as money lenders. Their venture capital paid for many high risk enterprises, including the establishment of the local rubber industry.

The temple is the focal point of the spectacular Thaipusam festival, not a sight for the squeamish, however, as devotees pierce their flesh with skewers and hooks, and carry huge metal frames called *Kavadis*. The festival takes place in January or February (see **Special Events**).
Less traumatic is the temple's Navarathi (nine nights) festival held in October when the temple is filled nightly with the sights and sounds of traditional Indian music and dance.
Temple open: daily, 08.00–12.00hrs, 17.30–20.30hrs.
MRT: Dhoby Ghaut
Bus: 123, 143

◆

CHINAMAN SCHOLARS GALLERY

148 Trengganu Street, Chinatown
Antique dealer Vincent Tan has created this museum in an old shop-house laid out as a typical pre-war Cantonese merchant/ scholar's home. He will explain the rituals associated with the tea ceremony and play some of the old musical instruments on display.
Open: Monday to Friday 09.00–16.00hrs (tel: 222 9554).
Bus: 124, 174, 190

◆◆◆
CHINATOWN ✓

Chinatown lies cheek by jowl with the towering skyscrapers of Singapore's financial district. Officially it is bounded by Cross Street to the north, New Bridge and South Bridge Roads to the west and east, and Cantonment Road to the south, a mere dozen streets with an area of just over three quarters of a square mile (2sq km). This forms the core of Chinatown, an area protected from development, but the area also includes Telok Ayer Street and Club Street on the eastern fringes, as well as the area north of Cross Road up to Boat Quay. Throughout Chinatown you will find run-down shop-houses, patched with bits of tin sheet and sprouting vegetation that has become embedded in the crumbling mortar. Shops spill out over the covered pavements, forcing pedestrians into the insalubrious gutters, while some crumbling buildings bear the hand-painted signs of hole-in-the-wall companies with grand names like Pacific Trading or Ocean Shipping. Despite its scruffiness, Chinatown continues to fascinate visitors. For some, the appeal is the architecture: capitals, pilasters, moulded plasterwork and cornices adorn the façades, painted in peeling pastel colours and some more than a century old. Others come to visit the temples, others to shop cheaply, and others to get a taste of Chinese life, peering inquisitively into the dark interiors of shop-houses with their heavy furnishings and altars to the gods of the home.
Chinatown was developed from the early 1840s, zoned as a settlement for Hokkien, Fukienese and Cantonese immigrants who arrived as

Shopping in Chinatown

indentured labourers, working in rubber plantations or harbour warehouses until they had paid off the cost of their passage. Many later became street hawkers, then restaurateurs; others specialised in crafts, jewellery making and tailoring, all industries that still thrive here. Earlier in the century, Chinatown had an extraordinarily dense population; one person to every 8 square feet (0.75sq m) of land, with whole families living in tiny airless cubicles. Today many Chinatown residents have been rehoused in more spacious Government flats.

Chinatown itself is officially a conservation area and, little by little, the old shop-houses are being restored. This is a difficult task because much of the property is privately owned and not everyone is willing to bear the cost; critics say that

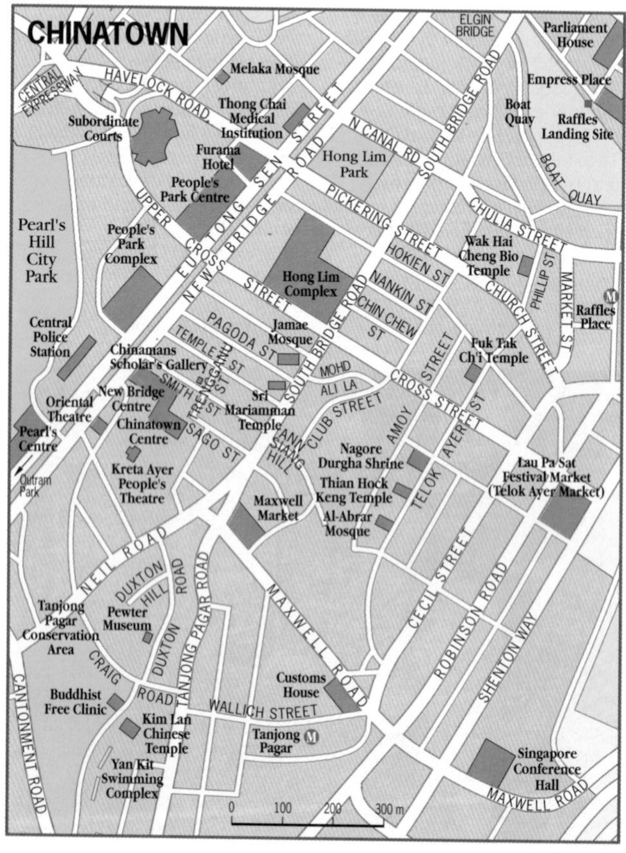

restoration has caused rents to rise, driving out the small businesses that lend the area so much character. To explore Chinatown walk from Raffles Place MRT station to Phillip Street, which once stood on the waterfront. The **Wak Hai Cheng Bio** (Temple of the Calm Sea) dates from 1852 and arriving immigrants would come here to give thanks for a safe passage. Chinese opera is performed in the courtyard on feast days.

On the banks of the Singapore River the old warehouses, *godowns* and shop-houses of **Boat Quay** have recently been restored and refurbished and now feature some 35 bars, restaurants and cafés, with al fresco dining on the water's edge one of the main attractions.

If you cross Church Street and head down Telok Ayer Street, you are still following the original waterfront. Several temples are strung along Telok Ayer Street, including the Nogore Durgha shrine, built by Indian Muslims in 1828; the **Fuk Tak Ch'i** Shenist temple and the **Thian Hock Keng** Hokkien temple (see separate entries). Return up Amoy Street where restoration work has returned some shop-houses to their original condition. Turn left in Cross Street and left again into Club Street. Linger here to watch woodcarvers turn blocks of wood into brightly-painted images of the many deities that populate the Chinese underworld, especially the house gods that hold pride of place in traditional kitchens. In Mohammad Ali Lane, linking Club Street and South Bridge Road, you will sometimes find a flea market in full swing. South Bridge Road is lined with jewellers' shops, incongruously partnered by the colourful **Sri Mariamman** Hindu shrine (see separate entry).

Wander up and down adjacent Temple Street and Sago Street. Sago Street still has a shop selling paper funerary figures of everything from money and gold credit cards to a Mercedes Benz or TV set, intended as offerings to the spirits. Families burn these offerings in temples or on the graves of their ancestors.

More restoration is going on in the Smith Street/Sago Street area, and both lanes run up to the Chinatown Centre where all the street hawkers now gather to sell their wares. The continuation of Smith Street, into New Bridge Road, is a good place to shop for T-shirts, kites, paper lanterns, fans, sunshades and umbrellas.

If you have any energy left, head back south along South Bridge Road to the junction of Neil Road and Tanjong Pagar Road. Here you will find the **Tanjong Pagar Restoration Area** where the colourful and ornate shop-houses have been turned into boutiques, restaurants and tea-houses. Alternatively, head back down New Bridge Street and cross the river to **Clarke Quay**; like Boat Quay, this old warehouse area has been comprehensively restored and developed and now features 176 air-conditioned shops, cafés, and bars, with outdoor food and produce stalls.

MRT: Raffles Place, Outram Park or Tanjong Pagar

Bus: 124, 167, 174, 179, 182, 190

Water Dragon at the Chinese Gardens, a haven of tranquility

◆

CHINESE AND JAPANESE GARDENS

Yuan Ching Road, Jurong

These two gardens lie side by side on two islands rising from the Jurong Lake, and are linked to each other by means of a bridge. The Chinese Garden embodies themes from the Beijing Summer Palace Gardens and the bold architectural forms of bridges, pavilions and pagodas are complemented by lotus-filled pools and areas devoted to scented plants and medicinal herbs as well as the Suzhou-style Penjing Garden with over 3,000 bonsai specimens. The simpler Japanese Garden is built around a carp pool with waterfalls and a Zen Garden of topiary and sculptural rocks. The best time to see the Chinese Garden is in mid-autumn Mooncake festival, when the islands and lake are festooned with lanterns and local children take part in traditional dances.

Open: daily, 09.00–18.00hrs (tel: 264 3455).

MRT: Chinese Garden

Bus: 198 to Boon Lay bus interchange, then 154

CITY HALL see **COLONIAL SINGAPORE**

◆◆◆
COLONIAL SINGAPORE ✓

At the heart of Singapore there is a broad expanse of green called the Padang (Malay for 'field'), surrounded by a group of stately colonial buildings that still serve their original function as the seat of government and justice. The history of Singapore is written in these buildings and, if you choose a viewpoint that blocks out the skyscrapers of the financial district on the other side of the river, you can easily imagine the appearance of Singapore in the 19th century (sadly, no viewpoint excludes the sight and sound of traffic).

If you start from City Hall MRT station, and turn your back on Raffles City Tower, the first building you see is **St Andrew's Cathedral**. This wedding-cake white, neo-gothic building was completed in 1862 and built by Indian convict labour. It is faced in Madras Churam, a plaster that incorporated shells, egg white and coconut fibres, said to be indestructible; in reality, the fabric lasted some 125 years in the equatorial climate before deterioration finally set in. It has now been fully restored to its former glory.

The 26-foot- (8m) high Merlion statue guards the bay

The **Padang** lies just across from the cathedral, alongside St Andrew's Road. From the earliest days of British rule in Singapore the Padang has been used for ceremonial parades and for the game that the British introduced to all their colonies – cricket. The **Singapore Cricket Club's** pavilion stands to the right of the Padang as you face the shore. You can watch cricket from the Padang most Saturday and Sunday afternoons from March until October (matches at 13.30hrs Saturday; 10.30hrs Sunday; tel: 338 9367 for information) but the Club pavilion is strictly for members and their guests. From November to March you are quite likely to see a game of rugby or hockey taking place here on a Saturday afternoon and the Padang is increasingly used for open-air entertainment. It is also the focal point of the National Day Parade which is held on 9 August.

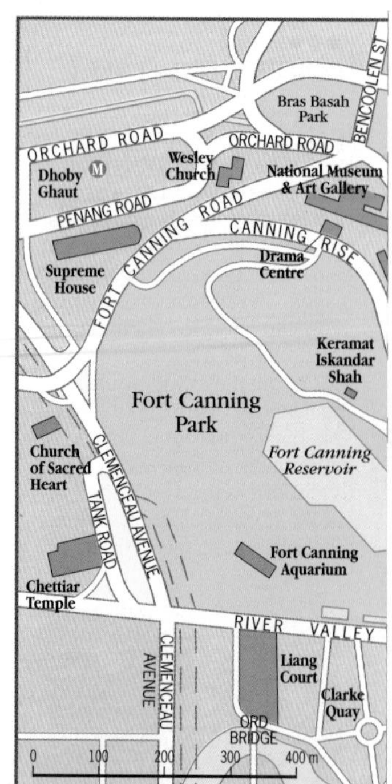

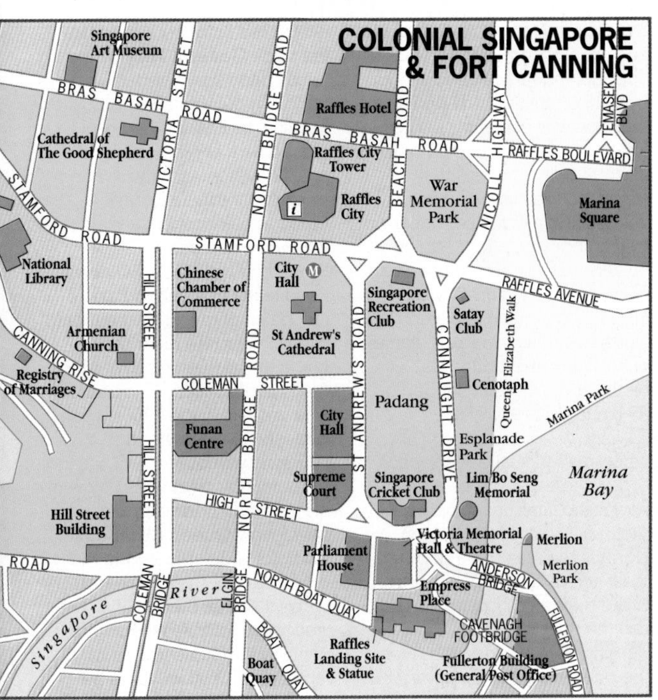

The attractive building at the opposite end of the Padang is the **Singapore Recreation Club**, founded in 1883; its members now include many of Singapore's top businessmen, civil servants and lawyers. Walking down St Andrew's Road towards the cricket pavilion, you pass **City Hall** on the right, with its imposing classical façade. The building was completed in 1929 and is home to various Government departments. However, the name is somewhat misleading, since Singapore does not have a separate municipal government; the name dates from 1952 when, as a step towards independence from British rule, the status of Singapore changed from that of Crown Colony to that of a 'City'. Next comes the **Supreme Court**, an elegant neo-classical building completed in 1939 and decorated with the seated figure of Justice carved by the Italian sculptor, Cavaliere Rodolfo Nolli. Crossing the High Street, walk down the narrow Parliament Lane to the riverside. On the right is **Parliament House**, an attractive Palladian-style building that was originally designed as a private mansion

Overlooking the Padang, the Singapore Cricket Club pavilion is still a members-only enclave

by George Drumgold Coleman, an Irish architect who served as Superintendent of Public Works from 1827 until the 1840s. The mansion was one of his earliest works; completed in 1827, it is also the oldest government building in Singapore. You can watch Parliament in session from the Strangers' Gallery (space is limited and it is best to reserve a place in advance on tel: 336 8811). Parliament Lane leads to North Boat Quay where a statue of **Sir Stamford Raffles** stands on the spot where he landed on 29 January 1819 to claim Singapore for the British. This whitewashed statue is a replica of the original bronze statue that now stands in front of the Victoria Theatre (see below). North Boat Quay has a good view across the Singapore River to the restored shop-houses that line the opposite bank.

Turning your back on the river, the bulky building on the right is **Empress Place Building**, built in 1864 and currently used for exhibitions of Asian art and culture (see separate entry). Alongside is the unmistakable clock tower that rises like a beacon between the classical porticoes of the **Victoria Theatre** and **The Victoria Memorial Hall**, the hubs of Singaporean theatrical and muscial life. The Memorial Hall, which opened in 1905, was built as a tribute to Queen Victoria, who died in 1901.

Close by is the attractive **Cavenagh Footbridge**, a pretty suspension bridge completed in 1869 in memory of the former Governor of Singapore, Major General Cavenagh. It leads across the Singapore River to the huge **General Post Office** (also called the Fullerton Building) completed in 1928. Massive as it is, it is dwarfed by the modern skyscrapers that now line Shenton Way, serving as offices for multinational banks, stock brokers and insurance companies.

From the Post Office, Fullerton Road leads to **Merlion Park,** a tiny patch of green by the mouth of the Singapore River, and home to a statue of the Merlion (half lion, half fish). This beast was created in the 1960s when it was felt the island needed a national symbol.

Crossing the river again by way of Anderson Bridge, you can now follow **Queen Elizabeth Walk** for a different perspective of Singapore's colonial heart, viewed across the Padang. The walk once followed the seafront until land reclamation left it landlocked. You will pass the pagoda-like **Lim Bo Seng Memorial**, commemorating a prominent leader of the resistance to Japanese occupation during World War II, and the **Cenotaph**, a memorial to the dead of both wars. An incongruous partner is the Satay Club, a popular hawker food centre.

Finally, as you return up Stamford Road to City Hall MRT station, the **War Memorial Park** stands to the right; the memorial with its four columns representing each of Singapore's main ethnic groups, commemorates local civilians who died under Japanese occupation.

MRT: City Hall

Underwater viewing areas allow close encounters with crocodiles

CROCODILE FARMS

Singapore has two farms where crocodiles are bred for their skins. Each has viewing areas and a shop selling reptile-skin products. A visit to the Jurong Crocodile Paradise could be combined with the nearby Jurong Birdpark.

Jurong Crocodile Paradise

241 Jalan Ahmad Ibrahim

Features over 2,500 fresh water and estuarine crocodiles in a landscaped setting, with underwater viewing areas and a breeding enclosure. The new Cavern of Darkness shows the nocturnal habits of the crocs.
Open: daily, 09.00–18.00hrs.
Wrestling shows 10.45, 11.45, 14.00, 15.00 and 16.00hrs.
MRT: Boon Lay Station then bus 251, 253 or 255
Bus: 198 to Boon Lay Bus interchange then 194 or 251

Singapore Crocodilarium

730 East Coast Parkway

Open: daily, 09.00–17.00hrs.
Feeding time Tuesday 11.00hrs (tel: 447 3722 for further information).
Wrestling shows 13.15 and 16.15hrs except Monday.
Bus: 14 to Katong Shopping Centre, then 25-minute walk to East Coast Parkway

EMPRESS PLACE BUILDING

Empress Place

Formerly used to house Government departments, this grandiose colonial building (completed in 1864) has been comprehensively restored and is used as a museum and exhibition space for Asian archaelogical and cultural material; exhibitions change from time to time but are well worth seeing, as they feature spectacular items on loan from some of Asia's leading museums.
Open: daily, 09.00–19.30hrs.
MRT: Raffles Place

FORT CANNING

Entrance on Canning Rise, alongside the National Library

Fort Canning is the name of the hill that sits at the centre of Fort Canning Park and is a very pleasant place to take a stroll. Lying just inside the neo-Gothic gateway to the park is a Christian cemetery with many old tombstones recording the dates and deeds of European settlers, including that of George Coleman, the architect of Parliament House and the Armenian Apostolic Church of St Gregory. Nothing now remains of the even older tombs of Malay princes who were buried here as early as the 14th century, though archaeological remains discovered during excavations on the hill are now displayed in the National Museum.

Fort Canning was the site of the very first British settlement in Singapore. Disregarding the fact that local people held the hill sacred, Sir Stamford Raffles had the jungle cleared and built his first residence and garden here. All that remains of the late 19th-century Fort Canning is the Fort Gate and two cannons; the military barracks (built in 1930) have been restored and now house the Singapore Dance Theatre, Theatreworks, the Black Box Theatre and an art gallery. Raffles' original 5-acre (19ha) 'experimental and botanical garden' (a precursor of the famous Botanic Gardens) has recently been recreated as a landscaped spice garden. The hill was also the site of an extensive underground bunker system which was used as the Far East Command and Control Centre during World War II.

MRT: City Hall

◆

FUK TAK CHI TEMPLE

76 Telock Ayer Street, Chinatown

You cannot miss this small temple because there are usually several Mercedes-Benz parked outside, a clue to the fact that the temple is sacred to the god of wealth. Successful businessmen make their offerings to the figure in sackcloth, with a chain of gold around his neck, who stands in the shadows to the left of the door, shrouded by the heavy smoke and scent of burning coils of incense. The shrine, whose name means 'Temple of Prosperity and Virtue' dates to 1825 and is one of the oldest in Singapore.

MRT: Raffles Place

Bus: 124, 167, 174, 179, 182, 190

GUINNESS WORLD OF RECORDS

02–70 World Trade Centre, 1 Maritime Square, off Telok Blangah Road

This clone of many exhibitions to be found all over the world makes concessions to its location by having a small section devoted to Singaporean and Asian record-breaking facts and feats. Otherwise it is the usual mixture of the fattest, biggest, heaviest, fastest and craziest things in the natural and human world. Children will love it. For information tel: 271 8344.

Open: daily and public holidays 09.30–20.30hrs.

MRT: Tanjong Pagar then taxi

Bus: 10, 30, 65, 97, 100, 143

♦♦♦
HARBOUR AND RIVER CRUISES ✓

From a boat you gain a different perspective of Singapore; the island's skyscrapers can look spectacular from the harbour and you will see something of the busy shipping lanes and ports that contribute so much to the local economy. You will also see some of the 57 smaller islands that make up the Singaporean archipelago, including some where modern life does not seem to have intruded; islands where the inhabitants still live in stilt houses built over the water and make their living from small-scale agriculture and fishing. There are two ways to explore Singapore by water: you can join one of the tours laid on by tour operators or you can hire your own so-called 'bumboat' (usually a converted lighter) and set your own itinerary. The former is by far the easier, since bumboat owners do not always speak good English and they may not turn out to be very communicative guides.
Harbour cruises can usually be booked in advance at your hotel travel desk. Some tickets may also be available at Clifford Pier, the departure point for all cruise operators, but advance booking is a safer bet.
All cruise operators follow more or less the same route, sailing through the southern straits for a view of the port and oil refineries and the islands of Sentosa, Kusu, Pulau Brani, Sisters' Island, St John's and Lazarus Island.

Cruises on the Singapore River are a popular way to explore the city, with skyscrapers providing the backdrop

'Short' cruises typically last an hour, while twilight dinner cruises last up to three hours. Prices vary according to the type of meal served at different times of day; lunch and twilight cruises are more expensive and include a buffet meal, while light refreshments are served during the morning and afternoon tours. The decision, therefore, comes down to the time of day you want to do the tour and type of boat.
The following company operates modern catamarans that can accommodate up to 200 passengers.
J & N Cruises (tel: 270 7100/278 4467).
Vessel: *Equator Triangle*; sailings 12.30, 15.00, 18.00, 20.30 and 22.30hrs (disco cruise).
Alternatively you can tour by motorised junk capable of carrying up to 100 passengers, operated by:
Watertours (tel: 533 9811).
Vessel: *Ann Heng*, *Cheng Ho*; sailings 10.30, 15.00, 18.00, 18.30hrs.

Eastwind (tel: 533 3432). Vessel: *Fairwind*; sailings 10.30, 15.00, 16.00, 18.00hrs.
If you can get together a group, you can also charter a motor yacht capable of carrying from 12 to 50 passengers. Chartering offers greater flexibility over timings and routes and some boats are equipped for longer, overnight trips to the coastal inlets and islands of Indonesia and Malaysia. Contact:
Fantasy Cruises (tel: 284 0424).
River cruises are offered by:
Singapore River Cruises (tel: 336 6119 or 227 6863).
Departure point: North Boat Quay. Operates every half hour between 09.00 and 19.00hrs.
Singapore Explorer (tel: 538 1677 or 336 6119).
Departure Point: Raffles Place/ Clarke Quay. Every half hour between 09.00 and 23.00hrs.

HAW PAR VILLA – DRAGON WORLD

262 Pasir Panjang Road

Haw Par Villa first opened its doors to the public in 1937 and the garden, full of extraordinary statues and scenes from Chinese mythology, has recently been restored to its full technicolour glory.
The villa is named after the two brothers who created it – Aw Boon Haw and Aw Boon Par. They inherited a fortune from their father who invented Tiger Balm ointment, still sold and widely regarded by Chinese people all over Asia as a universal panacea for all bodily ailments.
The brothers filled their garden with three-dimensional tableaux illustrating stories from Chinese legend that nearly all Chinese children learn at their mother's knee.
The new owners have turned the villa into a 23½-acre (9.5ha) theme park with special-effects theatres, Chinese pageants and flume rides, but the biggest draw still remains the grisly tableaux illustrating the punishments that await miscreants of all types once they reach the Courts of Hell in the Chinese underworld.
Open: daily, 09.00–18.00hrs (tel: 774 0300).
MRT: Buona Vista then bus 200
Bus: 10, 30, 51 and 143

Entering the dragons mouth: a mythical journey through the underworld at Haw Par Villa/ Dragon World

◆
INDONESIA

If you have exhausted Singapore's attractions, you can visit the nearby islands of **Batam** and **Bintan**, just two of the more than 17,000 islands that make up the Indonesian archipelago. Neither is an unspoilt Paradise, but both offer a contrast to the hubbub of Singapore. You can book day trips or two-day packages through most hotel travel desks and tour operators, or take a scheduled ferry service. Journey times are now much quicker thanks to a recently-opened new terminal, the Tanah Merah Ferry Terminal (TMFT), in the eastern part of Singapore; the ferry to Nongsapura (Batam) takes 40 minutes, and to Teluk Sebong (Bintan) one hour.

Day trips to the resorts of Batam are operated by the Batam View Beach Resort (tel: 276 8066), Grey Line Tours (tel: 331 8243), Singapore Sightseeing Tour Easy (tel: 332 3755), Holiday Tours (tel: 738 2622) and RMG Tours (tel: 738 7776).

The attractions on Bintan, 28 miles (45km) south east of Singapore, include clean and sheltered beaches, the Bintan Beach International Resort (currently being redeveloped as 'one of Asia's largest and most spectacular resorts'), and the markets and seafood stalls of the main town, Tanjung Pinang. Ferries depart from Singapore Monday to Thursday at 09.00, 12.30 and 15.30hrs, returning at 10.45, 14.15 and 18.15hrs. Friday to Sunday and Public holidays 09.00, 15.30 and 19.00hrs, returning at 14.15, 17.45 and 21.00hrs.

ISLANDS

Apart from Sentosa (see separate entry) the only islands served by scheduled ferry are Kusu and St John's. The ferry departs from the World Trade Centre, off Telok Blangah Road, and takes 30 minutes to reach Kusu and 60 minutes to St John's. There are only two sailings each day from Monday to Saturday: departing from the World Trade Centre at 10.00 and 13.30hrs; departing Kusu at 10.15, 11.45, 14.15 and 15.15hrs; departing St John's at 11.15 and 14.45hrs. On Sundays and public holidays the services are more frequent: departing the World Trade Centre at 09.45, 11.15, 12.45, 14.15, 15.45 and 17.15hrs; departing Kusu at 10.20, 11.50, 13.20, 14.50, 16.20 and 17.50hrs; departing St John's at 10.35, 12.05, 13.35, 15.05, 16.35 and 18.05hrs. Both islands have clean swimming beaches but they do become crowded at weekends. Kusu island also has two small shrines, the Tua Pek Kong Chinese temple on the beach and a Malay shrine to Abdul Rahman on the island's peak. Both are centres of pilgrimage, especially during the ninth lunar month of the Chinese calendar (usually October) when the ferries are full to capacity.

Spectacular displays with trained birds of prey at the Jurong Bird Park

The pilgrimage commemorates, in part, the fusion of the Malay and Chinese people that characterises Singaporean society. According to legend Kusu was formed when a giant turtle was transformed into an island so as to rescue two drowning sailors – one Malay, one Chinese – who became sworn brothers; hence the island's name (Kusu is Malay for turtle).

◆◆◆

JURONG BIRD PARK ✓

Jurong Hill, Jalan Ahmad Ibrahim

Jurong Bird Park was established in 1971 and has become one of Singapore's most popular attractions. The park has over 8,000 birds from all over the world, housed in landscaped enclosures or spacious aviaries. The largest aviary covers 5 acres (2ha) and encloses a jungle, complete with waterfall, in which tropical birds fly at will. Highlights include the world's largest collection of Southeast Asian Hornbills and South American Toucans, and over 200 penguins in the Penguin Parade enclosure. Daily shows include Breakfast with the Birds, Birds of Prey in which trained birds are put through their paces during the day (tel: 261 8866), Penguin Feeding and an All-Star Bird Show (tel: 265 0022 for times). The best introduction to the park is to take the monorail (which even goes through some aviaries) and then to walk round.
Open: Monday to Friday 09.00–18.00hrs; Saturday, Sunday and public holidays 08.00–18.00hrs.
MRT: Boon Lay Station then bus 251, 253 or 255

◆

KRANJI WAR MEMORIAL

Mandai Road/Woodlands Road junction

This memorial to Allied troops who lost their lives in the defence and occupation of Singapore during World War II is set in a peaceful park north of the island.
Bus: 182, 170

◆◆◆
LITTLE INDIA ✓

Little India spreads up Serangoon Road from its junction with Bukit Timah Road and spills into the narrow streets either side. Serangoon Road is a busy traffic thoroughfare, but the traders who operate out of hole-in-the-wall cubicles and shop-houses seem oblivous to the traffic and, as you walk under the awnings that project over the narrow pavement, the atmosphere is that of the sub-continent. The area is permeated by the smells of pungent spices and you can watch them being milled by men in *dhotis* and converted into packages of brightly coloured powders. Alongside you will find shops piled so high with bolts of brightly coloured fabrics that there scarcely seems room for customers to enter, and the pavements are crowded with stall holders selling Indian movie magazines, sweets, sandals, and garlands of fragrant jasmine and marigold flowers.

Large-scale development of Little India really began in the 1920s and you can still see some of the earliest buildings, decorated with art nouveau tiles, columns, swags, garlands and louvre windows, in Upper Weld Road. The back streets leading off Serangoon Road are lively with hundreds of pavement businesses engaged in everything from jewellery making and tailoring to metal-bashing and vehicle repairs. Once rather down-at-heel, Little India has recently been extensively renovated. Some of its best shops are now grouped in the Little India Arcade, just off Serangoon Road.

MRT: Bugis
Bus: 64, 65, 106, 111

Convict Beginnings

The Indians of Singapore have played a formative role in the creation of the island State: British-educated Indians were encouraged to settle here and work as civil servants by Sir Stamford Raffles. Raffles also used Indian convict labour to clear the island's mangrove swamps and build roads and public utilities. Convicts drafted to work in Singapore were treated well by the standards of the time. They were held at a prison near Serangoon Road and, once their sentence was over, were given land nearby to farm; thus the area developed its distinctive Indian character.

Hindu temples are rich in colourful ornamentation, such as this figure of a deity

A far cry from the rush of Singapore, Malacca's waterfront is a haven of peace and quiet

♦♦♦ MALAYSIA ✓

The southern tip of peninsular Malaysia is only a short bus- or taxi-ride away from Orchard Road. All you need to enter the country is a passport valid for at least six months beyond the date of entry.

Tour operators and hotel travel desks all offer low-cost, half- or full-day coach excursions and longer packages for those with the time to travel north to Malacca or Penang. It is best to choose a weekday for your excursion since the causeway linking Singapore to Malaysia is very busy at weekends and queuing to cross will eat into the time you have available to explore the peninsula. If you want to go it alone, you can take bus 170, which leaves Queen Street or Bukit Timah Road every 15 minutes; or take the Johor Bahru express bus which leaves the Ban San Street terminus every 10 minutes. The fare costs a few cents and the journey time to Johor Bahru is just over 30 minutes.

Johor Bahru lies immediately the other side of the ¾-mile- (1km) long causeway that crosses the Strait of Johor. The town was founded in 1855 as the new capital of the sultanate of Johor. Highlights include the Abu Bakar

Mosque, built in 1892, and the nearby Istana Besar, built in 1866 as a royal residence and surrounded by public gardens (both located in Jalan Abu Bakar, the road that runs parallel to the Strait of Johor).
Further inland is Malacca, a fascinating town whose architecture reflects a long history of settlement by the Portuguese, Dutch, English and Chinese. There are also numerous antique shops – though you will not find any bargains. Malacca is some 150 miles (240km) from Singapore and if you take a day trip you will spend 10 hours on the coach and only two hours in the town; consequently it is better to take a two-day package.

◆
MANDAI ORCHID GARDENS

Mandai Lake Road
A visit to the Mandai Orchid Gardens can be combined with a visit to the **Zoo** next door. These gardens are a showcase for the many spectacular orchid varieties that have been introduced to Singapore or produced here by hybridisation and which are now produced on a commercial scale for sale to florists throughout Singapore and for export worldwide. The garden was created by John Laycock and Lee Kim Hong in 1950, and together they virtually created today's orchid industry. The garden itself is beautifully landscaped and you will always find a spectacular display of colourful flowers, whatever the time of year (tel: 269 1036).
Open: daily, 08.30–17.30hrs.
Bus: 171 or take the Zoo Express coach service which calls at major hotels (for information tel: 235 3111).

MERLION PARK see **COLONIAL SINGAPORE**

Water lilies in the Mandai Orchid Gardens

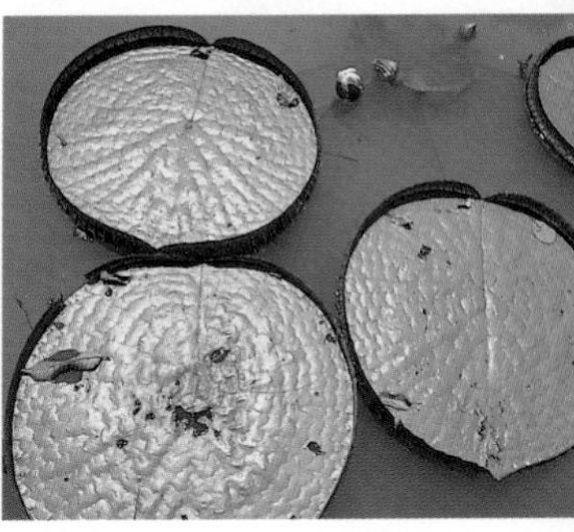

♦♦♦
NATIONAL MUSEUM ✓

Stamford Road
The classical, domed building that houses the National Museum is one of Singapore's finest examples of colonial architecture. The museum, built in honour of Queen Victoria's Golden Jubilee, opened in 1887. The ground floor features a series of small-scale dioramas that vividly illustrate the appearance of colonial Singapore, the crowded interiors of houses in Chinatown, and the meeting of Singapore's first Parliament following independence in 1965. The upper floor has reconstructions, with taped commentaries, on Malay, Chinese and Indian wedding ceremonies, the entire furnishings of a fashionable Straits-Chinese house, and a large collection of jade and ceramics. A new addition is a Children's Discovery Gallery, with interactive exhibits on the city's cultural heritage, visual and performing arts. The museum is linked to the adjacent Art Gallery, featuring temporary exhibitions drawn from the gallery's permanent collection as well as commercial exhibitions by local artists and societies.
Open: daily, except Monday, 09.00–16.30hrs.
MRT: City Hall or Dhoby Ghaut

PADANG, THE see **COLONIAL SINGAPORE**

PARLIAMENT HOUSE see **COLONIAL SINGAPORE**

The Art Gallery is housed in an elegant former hotel

♦♦
PERANAKAN SHOWHOUSE MUSEUM

Emerald Hill, 180 Orchard Road
Of all the ethnic groups that live in Singapore, the Straits-Chinese have always regarded themselves as something special – almost a noble caste, with their own distinctive language, cuisine, architecture, dress and customs. Straits-Chinese continue to populate the upper echelons of business, law and administration in Singapore though much of their culture – with the exception of their cooking – is now a subject for museum displays such as the one at this excellent reconstruction of a typical Straits-Chinese house.
The Peranakan Showhouse Museum displays fine examples of Straits-Chinese furniture, embroidery and porcelain. The house itself is one of a row of terraced houses with lavishly-

Straits-Chinese
The Straits-Chinese community evolved from early Chinese traders who settled in Singapore and the coastal parts of Malaysia, intermarrying with local Malays. They are variously known as Peranakans (meaning 'local born'), Babas, after their language which evolved, over several centuries, as a fusion of Malay and Chinese, or Nonyas, after their cuisine which incorporates Malay spices. Later, the Straits-Chinese absorbed elements of British culture and proved such conscientious supporters of the colonial administration that they earned yet another name – the King's Chinese.

Seated Buddha, Sakya Muni Temple

decorated façades that illustrate Straits-Chinese eclecticism and love of ornament. The museum forms part of a complex incorporating the Keday Kopi coffee shop (*open*: Monday to Friday 10.30–15.30hrs).
MRT: Somerset

◆◆
RAFFLES HOTEL

Beach Road
Raffles Hotel is virtually synonymous with Singapore. Who has not heard of the 'Grand Old Lady of the East', the haunt of Kipling, Conrad and Somerset Maugham, or of 'Singapore Sling', the cocktail invented here by barman Ngiam Tong Boon in 1915 (a blend of gin, cherry brandy, Angostura bitters, Cointreau, Benedictine and fruit juice). Such is the worldwide fame of Raffles that by the late 1980s the hotel had deteriorated into a travesty of its former glory, more concerned with serving Slings by the bucketful to bus loads of tourists than with giving the service that once attracted the great and famous. However, the hotel, which saw its first guests in 1887, has been entirely restored and expanded, and now includes an arcade with 70 shops. On the first floor there is also a little museum, displaying the hotel's illustrious past, with fascinating travel memorabilia (such as old posters, luggage labels and period photographs).
Museum open: daily, 10.00–21.00hrs.
MRT: City Hall

ST ANDREW'S CATHEDRAL
see **COLONIAL SINGAPORE**

◆◆
SAKYA MUNI TEMPLE (TEMPLE OF A THOUSAND LIGHTS)

Race Course Road
This extraordinary temple was built entirely by the Buddhist monk Vutthisasara who came to Singapore from Thailand at the turn of the century and devoted his life to the teaching of Buddhist principles. At the focal point of the temple, which was built in the style of a *wat* or monastery, there is a huge seated figure of Buddha, nearly 50 feet (15m) high and weighing 300 tons, surrounded by a nimbus of lights – hence the temple's popular name. Scenes from the life of Buddha are painted around the base of the statue.
Open: 07.00–16.45hrs.
Bus: 111, 106, 65, 64

The Musical Fountain is just one attraction on the 'fun island' of Sentosa

◆◆◆
SENTOSA ISLAND ✓

The island of Sentosa lies immediately south of Singapore, separated by a ¼-mile (0.5km) wide stretch of water.
Conversion of the island from a military base into a playground for some 2 million visitors a year began in the 1970s and today the attractions include museums, gardens and a series of beaches and leisure lagoons. It would take the best part of a day to explore all of Sentosa's attractions; or you could just go for an evening to watch the musical fountain.
The most scenic way to reach Sentosa is on the cable car from Mount Faber; it operates daily from 08.30–21.30hrs. Alternatively, you can take the Sentosa ferry from the World Trade Centre, which operates daily from 10.00–21.00hrs. Since the opening of a causeway across to the island, there are also bus services from the World Trade Centre, Orchard Road and Tiong Bahru MRT, which operate every 10–15 minutes. You can also get there by taxi, on foot or by bicycle.
The basic admission charge to Sentosa is S$5, with combined tickets also available for the internal monrail and some of the attractions.
Sentosa has four museums which trace the history of Singapore from different aspects. **Pioneers of Singapore** and the **Surrender**

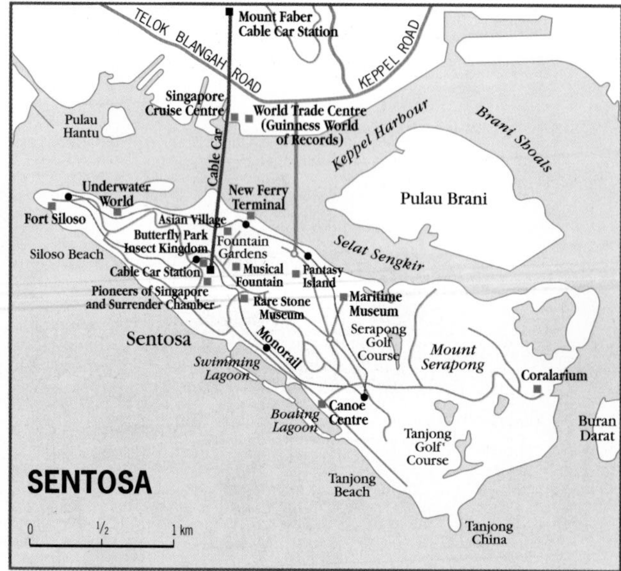

Chambers both use waxwork tableaux, taped commentaries and other media to tell the story of the founding of the British colony and of the Japanese occupation during World War II.

The **Maritime Museum** traces the history of the port with some fine models of junks and early sailing ships. **Fort Siloso** on the eastern tip of the island is the only preserved fort (dating back to 1880) in Singapore, and features tunnels, guns and a new 'sensory experience' of life as a recruit.

Attractions centred on the natural world include the excellent **Underwater World** aquarium (one of the largest in Asia, with some 5,000 species), the **Butterfly Park** and **Insect Kingdom Museum**, a **Rare Stone Museum**, a **Coralium**, and various gardens including the **Fountain Gardens**, a **Flower Terrace**, **Orchid Fantasy**, and a **Dragon Trail** through the jungle.

The ever-expanding range of things to see and do on Sentosa also includes an **Asian Village**, the **Lost Civilisation/Ruined City**, a new **Volcanoland** multi-media experience which includes a simulated journey through the earth's core, and the new **Fantasy Island**, Asia's largest water theme park, with 32 water attractions and slides.

◆◆

SINGAPORE ART MUSEUM

71 Bras Basah Road

Housed in a beautifully restored school building (the former St Joseph's Institution, the first Catholic school in Singapore),

the new national art gallery showcases contemporary art from Singapore and Southeast Asia. One of the main attractions is the E-mage Gallery which features interactive programmes of contemporary works on large, high definition monitors.
Open: daily, 09.00–17.30hrs.
Closed: Monday.
MRT: Dhoby Ghaut or City Hall

◆◆
SINGAPORE SCIENCE CENTRE
Science Centre Road, Jurong
Science education has a high priority in Singapore which has an industry-based economy. The Science Centre is where large (and often noisy) groups of schoolchildren come to learn about fundamental principles, from the circulation of blood to the dynamics of flight. Set in four themed galleries, the museum boasts such state-of-the-art attractions as hands-on computers, laser displays, a walk-through model of the human body and the purpose-built Crazy Room, where you can explore the effects of scientific principles and have fun doing so! If this is of no interest to you, at least consider seeing a three-dimensional film at the Centre's Omnimax cinema, with its huge hemispherical screen.
Open: daily, except Monday, 10.00–18.00hrs. Films are changed regularly in the Omnimax cinema: for programme details, tel: 560 3316.
MRT: Jurong East then bus 336
Bus: 51, 66, 97, 197 and 336

SINGAPORE WAR MEMORIAL
see **COLONIAL SINGAPORE**

◆◆
SIONG LIM TEMPLE
184-E Jalan Toa Payoh
This huge and colourful Buddhist temple was founded at the turn of the century but has gone on growing ever since. It is built in traditional Chinese style modelled, in part, on the buildings of Beijing's Forbidden City.
MRT: Toa Payoh and then by taxi (no buses).

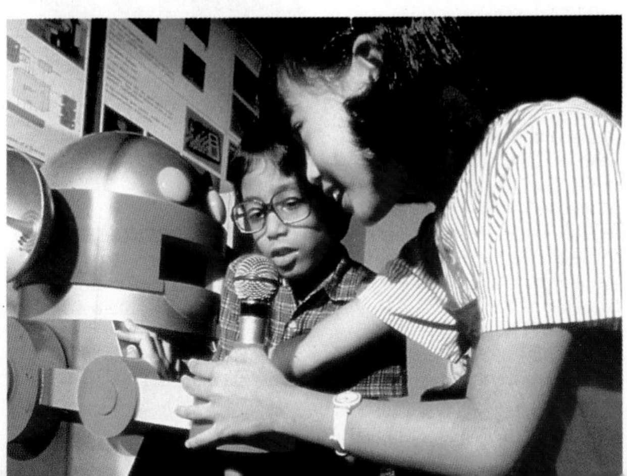

Hands-on, interactive exhibits are a highlight of the Science Centre

SRI MARIAMMAN TEMPLE

244 South Bridge Road

The polychromatic *gopuram* (gateway) to this shrine, with scenes from Hindu mythology, forms an exotic contrast to the nearby shopping complexes of South Bridge Road. The temple, restored several times, dates back to the 1860s in its present form and was originally founded in the 1820s. The interior shrines are covered in colourful scenes from the lives of Hindu deities and the sense of mystery is heightened by the traditional music that accompanies the temple ceremonies held every evening, starting at 18.00hrs. The temple is best seen during the Festival of Thimithi (October or November) when devotees test their faith by walking across red-hot coals.

Bus: 124, 174

SUPREME COURT see **COLONIAL SINGAPORE**

TANG DYNASTY CITY

2 Yuan Ching Road, Jurong

Asia's largest cultural theme park, Tang Dynasty City is a recreation of the 7th-century capital of China, Chang-An. It includes displays of over 100 life-sized models of famous Chinese figures (from Genghis Khan to Mao Zedong), a five-storey pagoda, an underground palace with over 1,000 terracotta replicas of the Xian warriors, a spine-chilling Chinese Ghost Mansion, and a Silk Road 'open city' with calligraphers, tea-houses and potteries.

Open: daily, 09.30–18.00hrs.

MRT: Lakeside, then bus 154, 240

Gopuram, Sri Mariamman Temple

THIAN HOCK KENG TEMPLE

Telok Ayer Street

If you visit only one temple in Singapore, this would be a good one to choose, for it is one of the island's oldest, largest and liveliest Chinese shrines.

The temple was built in 1840 on what was then the waterfront and dedicated to Ma Chu Po, goddess of the sea. At first sight the temple, with its prow-shaped roof ridges decorated with curving dragons, looks purely Chinese. Closer inspection reveals, however, a fine set of cast-iron railings, imported from Scotland, that run the length of the temple façade and numerous ceramic tiles set into the walls that were made in England and the Netherlands. Door gods, painted in splendid colours and picked out in gold, guard the high threshold, designed to trip up any evil spirits.
MRT: Raffles Place
Bus: 124, 167, 174, 179, 182, 190

Temple Rituals
It is well worth standing and watching the rituals observed by visitors to the Chinese temples; supplicants will buy a bunch of joss sticks and progress round the temple complex, standing for a moment in front of each shrine to pray and leave one stick from the bundle before they move on. Others purchase paper bundles on which are painted prayers, wishes and promises – requests for the help of the gods in achieving some desired objective – which are burnt, the smoke and flames carrying the message to the spirit world. Such practices are as old as the temple itself, but modern innovations are in evidence as well: these days the temple's fortune-telling service is all done by computer!

VICTORIA THEATRE see **COLONIAL SINGAPORE**

◆

FORT CANNING AQUARIUM

Fort Canning Park, entrance from River Valley Road
Over 500 species of marine creatures from tropical and temperate waters are on display in this rather dated museum.
Open: daily, 09.00–21.30hrs.
MRT: City Hall
Bus: 32

♦♦♦
ZOOLOGICAL GARDENS ✓

80 Mandai Lake Road
Singapore was one of the pioneers of the open zoo concept and the Zoological Gardens, established in 1973, consist of a series of park and jungle enclosures where the animals have plenty of freedom to roam and graze, separated from the public by means of moats, banks or walls. The zoo specialises in Southeast Asian species, including Komodo Dragons, orang-utans and tigers and houses more than 2,000 animals. New exhibits include Snake Encounters (an aviary-style exhibit with free-ranging snakes) and an African Lion enclosure with a glass-fronted viewing gallery.
Open: daily, 08.30–18.00hrs.
MRT: Yishun Station then by bus 171.
The Zoo Express Coach picks up and drops off visitors staying at major hotels (for further information tel: 235 3111).

Hippos are amongst more than 2,000 animals at the zoo

PEACE AND QUIET

Wildlife and Countryside in Singapore by Paul Sterry

Singapore lies off the southern tip of Malaysia, separated from the mainland by the Straits of Johor and from Indonesia by the Straits of Singapore. Lying less than 90 miles (145km) north of the equator, the climate is equatorial, with the oceanic influence of the sea moderating any extremes. Day length and daily temperature maximums of around 30°C/86°F vary little throughout the year. Relative humidity is more or less constant and rainfall is high throughout the year, although July is comparatively dry. Thunderstorms are a spectacular, and sometimes daily, occurrence.

The island is comparatively low-lying: Bukit Timah, the highest point, is only 533 feet (162.5m) above sea level. A century or so ago, the whole of the island, with the exception of the coastal fringe and wetland areas, would have been covered in tropical rainforest. In common with developing areas around the world, however, the story today is rather different. Apart from a few protected areas, the primary forest (areas where the trees have never been felled) has gone, either cut for timber and firewood or cleared for development and farming. Nevertheless, many of Singapore's plants and animals are hardy and adaptable, and there is never any shortage of things to see.

Urban Areas, Parks and Gardens

Wildlife interest is not confined to the remnants of natural vegetation and nature reserves. To the credit of the Singapore authorities, who were concerned about the alarming urbanisation of this tiny island, a policy of tree planting and 'greening' is now in force. Newly built-up areas are invariably decorated with shrubs and trees and these soon attract native birds and a range of climbing and epiphytic plants. There are also parks and gardens, several extensive, and the Botanic Gardens are renowned both as a haven of tranquillity and as a site of wildlife interest.

Labrador Nature Reserve Park and Fort Canning are worth exploring, and the paths and trails through the reservoir parks of Seletar – Lower Pierce, Upper Pierce and MacRitchie – in the centre of Singapore Island, can be good: lucky visitors may see mousedeer and skinks. Colourful butterflies abound and the birdlife is rich. The Singapore Zoological Gardens are near by. The Botanic Gardens, established in 1859, are on Cluny Road. In addition to a small area of natural rainforest there are cultivated orchids (the collection is world famous), giant fan palms, cycads, and many more introduced species from around the world – 2,000 species in all. The waterside settings are peaceful and undeniably attractive. Look for reticulated pythons, tree shrews and long-tailed macaques in the more wooded areas.

Around the Coast

Although development and land reclamation have destroyed many of Singapore's coastal habitats, there are still mangroves, mudflats, sandy beaches and rocky shores to be found. The offshore islands are less developed and a few of them have rich and colourful coral reefs.

To developers' eyes, estuaries and mudflats may appear waste areas ripe for reclamation, but for waterbirds they are vital feeding grounds. Many of the species can feed nowhere else: destroy the mudflats and you lose the birds. The surface layers of the mud are rich in organic matter and support vast numbers of marine worms and crustaceans; it is these which attract the birds.

Birds of Parks and Gardens
Yellow vented bubul
Black-naped oriole
Pink-necked pigeon
Brahminy kite
Common iora
Common myna
Flyeater
Tree sparrow
Brown-throated sunbird
Crested treeswift
Palm swift
Richard's pipit
Collared kingfisher
White-throated kingfisher
Grey heron
Cinnamon bittern
Philippine starling

One of the best areas of estuary and mudflats is the Serangoon estuary in northeast Singapore, which can be reached via Tampines Road near the Serangoon Sewage Works. Sad to say, even this outstanding spot is under threat.

Abandoned prawn ponds, such as those at Sungei Buloh in northern Lim Chu Kang, are also good for birds. Most of the species of wader found on the mudflats are also found on the prawn ponds in varying numbers, and herons, egrets and kingfishers are ever present. The few remaining areas of sandy beach also attract birds, although in lesser numbers and variety than the estuaries.

Take the monorail for a bird's eye view of the Jurong Bird Garden

Mangroves, which are such a feature of tropical coastal waters around the world, are a fascinating habitat. The trees here are superbly adapted to this challenging environment: for several hours a day their roots are submerged in salt water and in choking, anaerobic mud. The exposed parts of the root systems take in air at low tide and effectively 'breathe' for the roots as a whole.

Mangroves are extremely significant to the ecology of tropical coasts. The tangled network of roots gradually silts up and creates new land, advancing into the sea each year. The sheltered backwaters created by mangrove creeks serve as important nurseries for fish and crustaceans and the silt deposits are home to fiddler crabs, pistol prawns and mudskippers. These in turn are food for collared kingfishers, egrets and herons. Not so long ago, a good deal of the shoreline was fringed with mangrove forests. With increasing needs for stakes, firewood and charcoal, the mangroves were gradually felled and, in more recent years, have provided land suitable for reclamation and development. The last remaining mangroves of any note are found near the mouths of the Seletar and Serangoon estuaries.

If you have the opportunity to visit a coral reef off one of the islands to the south of Singapore, it will be well worth the effort. Corals require comparatively clear water – silt soon chokes and kills them – and so only certain areas are suitable for reefs to develop. Look for brain corals, starfish, sea urchins, rays, sharks and clownfish near to the surface: masks and snorkels are a 'must'.

Wetlands

Most of Singapore's wetland habitats have been modified in one way or another. However, freshwater animals are surprisingly adaptable and the waters of the island's ponds and ditches often teem with life. To satisfy the thirst of Singapore's human population, several large reservoirs have been constructed. These have inadvertently added significantly to the freshwater habitats available for colonisation. Four reservoirs – Seletar, Lower Pierce, Upper Pierce and MacRitchie – are found in the centre of the island, while Kranji Reservoir – the best aquatic area – lies in the northwest of the island.

At Kranji, mangroves and open sea can be seen from the dam, over which the road crosses, but the best areas of fresh water are seen from the vicinity of the pumping station on the reservoir's southern shores. Look and listen for great reed warblers and fan-tailed warblers, and scan the vegetated margins for purple herons, cinnamon bitterns, yellow bitterns and kingfishers. In the waters are pond tortoises, frogs, toads and fish.

Tropical Rainforests

In rainforests the vegetation grows on a grand scale: huge trees tower above the forest floor and twisted and contorted climbing plants fight their way to the tree canopy. Not surprisingly, the forests which once cloaked Singapore were soon felled for timber, firewood and land development.

However, a 10-acre (4ha) plot is maintained in the Botanic Gardens, while the best area – 185 acres (60ha) – is in the Bukit Timah Nature Reserve to the southwest of the reservoir parks. This reserve is a poignant reminder of the wonderful forest that once covered the island.

The diversity of plant and animal life in the rainforest is astonishing. In an area of just a few acres, several hundred species of trees may occur, with two individuals of the same species seldom growing side by side. Contrast this with a temperate woodland in Europe or North America, which may comprise one dominant species of tree with a mosaic of perhaps five or six other species interspersed.

First impressions are usually of the deep shade and the tranquillity. In response to the shallow soils, most of the tall trees have developed immense buttress roots which provide support and stability. In addition to the climbing plants and strangler figs, many of the forest plants are epiphytic – that is, they grow not in the ground but on the branches and trunks of the trees. The orchids of tropical rainforests are renowned for this way of life. Having absorbed the scale and majesty of the forest, initial attempts at observing its resident wildlife may prove rather frustrating. The light is poor and

Brahminy kite in flight

creatures tend to be rather shy or retiring. Early mornings are best for the birds: they are at their most active then and can sometimes be located by song or call. Walk quietly along forest trails listening for rustling among the leaves or for noisy mixed flocks which may pass by from time to time. Colourful and exotic insects and other invertebrates will not be hard to find, but the forest mammals may be rather

Bird Migration

Many species that breed in northern Asia and move south to escape harsh winters, avoid flying directly over the sea by passing down the Malaysian peninsula and Indonesian archipelago. Singapore's geographical position at the southern tip of the Malaysian peninsula makes it of extreme strategic importance to these migrants, providing a land base for feeding and resting.

The migrant birds time their arrival and departure at their breeding grounds in Asia to maximise the favourable weather and good feeding. This means that Singapore receives visitors heading north from March to May, with the return passage occurring during September and October. Some of the autumn migrants may even remain on Singapore for the winter. Being large, diurnal migrants, birds of prey such as honey-buzzards and Japanese sparrowhawks are sometimes seen circling overhead.

Around the coast, look for flocks of migrant waders such as curlew, sandpipers, whimbrels and red-necked stints. These birds migrate at night and feed on the mudflats during the day. Migrant songbirds, such as flycatchers, shrikes, warblers and swallows, may stop off in parks, gardens, forests or, indeed, anywhere that provides a chance to rest and feed.

Bukit Timah Nature Reserve is covered by the last remaining area of tropical rainforest in Singapore

more of a challenge. Tree shrews, pangolins, flying lemurs and flying squirrels are occasionally seen.

Agricultural Land and Secondary Forest

Much of the land cleared of its rainforest cover by early settlers was turned over to agriculture. The technique of slash-and-burn produced a brief flush of fertility in the soil and led to today's patterns of neat, tended fields and abandoned plots. Characteristic crops include tapioca, sweet potatoes and aubergines, as well as many other species which have persisted from early farming practices. In such a lush environment, it is not surprising that 'nature' soon encroaches on this agricultural land once it is abandoned. Grasses and sedges soon take over and eventually a secondary forest, called *belukar*, develops. Although it may lack the diversity of true rainforest, *belukar* woodland is nevertheless good for wildlife. It has the added benefit that its resident creatures are comparatively easy to see in what is a more open habitat. Look for squirrels, tortoises and fruit bats among the *Albizia* trees, figs, huge ferns and rhododendrons.

FOOD AND DRINK

Food is, arguably, Singapore's number one attraction. Nowhere else in Asia – with the exception of Hong Kong – will you find such a diversity of ethnic cuisines, such freshness of ingredients and such flair in the presentation of dishes, all of which make eating out in Singapore a continuous adventure.

The sheer number of eating establishments is a testimony to the Singaporean national obsession with food. It has been estimated that it would take someone nearly 20 years to eat in every food outlet in Singapore, working at a steady rate of three meals a day.

Good food is also surprisingly cheap. For the price that many an overseas visitor may pay back home for a lunchtime snack, a Singaporean office worker can sit down to a feast of barbecued chicken, pork or fish with rice and a wholesome broth of meat stock and shredded vegetables.

You will not be able to enjoy the full variety of Singaporean cuisine on a short visit unless you team up with friends and eat as a group – eight is the optimum number and four the minimum, if you are to do justice to the range of tasty dishes on offer.

The idea is to order several dishes and share them, taking a morsel from each dish and enjoying the whole spectrum of contrasts in flavour, texture and

The local cuisine is cosmopolitan – and includes satay from Indonesia

spiciness, rather than limiting your scope to the monotony of a single dish. By sharing in this way you can sample perhaps six or eight different dishes at a sitting without adding inches to your waistline or feeling incapacitated for the rest of the day.

You do not need to order an expensive bottle of wine to accompany your meal if you are eating Asian food; the traditional accompaniment is tea – especially the fragrant and easily digested jasmine tea – although mineral water or freshly squeezed fruit juice are equally enjoyable and popular nowadays.

Do not be put off if some of the restaurants recommended here have rather an unpromising décor. The idea of rating a restaurant on the basis of its linen, carpets and curtains is wholly alien to the Asian gourmet – what matters is the quality of the food and some of the island's best restaurants are exceedingly plain. They can also be noisy, lively places, quite unlike the hushed dining rooms of the West.

Eating in Singapore is a celebration of the good things in life; everyone joins in the fun, from grandmother to the youngest children, especially on Sundays when it is traditional for families to go out together for lunch.

Local Food

It is not easy, even for Singaporeans, to define local food (in the sense of dishes that are peculiarly Singaporean), since the island's cuisine has absorbed so many different influences from other countries – principally from China, Malaysia and Indonesia.

Singapore noodles and Hainanese chicken have, at various times, been promoted as the national dishes of Singapore and you will find them on just about every hotel coffee-shop menu. Neither is a gourmet experience, although Hainanese chicken, poached and served with rice, cucumbers, chicken broth and three sauces – soy, chilli and ginger – is at least nourishing, cheap and popular. Moreover, it is one of the few dishes that all Singaporeans – except for vegetarians – can eat without transgressing ethnic or religious dietary laws.

For something that is both indigenous and unusual, most Singaporeans would point to Nonya cuisine, though they would also add that the best Nonya dishes can only be sampled in the home. Indeed, until the late 1970s you could only taste Nonya food by befriending a Straits-Chinese and securing a dinner invitation, and it is only recently that specialist restaurants have begun to open.

Nonya food evolved, like the Straits-Chinese themselves, from the inter-marriage of Chinese and Malay ingredients. Characteristic dishes include a rich casserole of chicken and *buah keluak* nuts, called *ayam buah keluak*; a stew of pork or

Colourful Nonya cakes taste delicious

Puddings can trip the light fantastic

beef with bamboo shoots and mushrooms called *babipong tay*; fish, pork and beancurd balls in clear soup, called *pon tauhu*; fish cooked in banana leaf – *otak otak*; spring rolls – *popiah*; and *laksa lemak* – noodles in a rich and spicy coconut-based soup.

To sample Nonya cuisine, try the following:

Nonya & Baba Restaurant, 262 River Valley Road (tel: 734 1382). Regarded as serving the best and most authentic Nonya cuisine in Singapore. Straits-Chinese costumes, dowry baskets and family photographs decorate the walls and proof of the quality of the food is the number of local Straits-Chinese who eat here regularly. *Open*: daily, from 11.30hrs. Last orders 21.45hrs. Inexpensive.

Peranakan Inn, 210 East Coast Road (tel: 440 6195). Another restaurant sought out by locals for its authentic traditional food. *Open*: daily, 11.00–15.00hrs and 18.00–23.30hrs. Inexpensive.

Malay/Indonesian Food

Singaporeans tend to regard Malay and Indonesian food as one cuisine – using Malay in the generic, rather than the narrowly nationalistic sense – and they are perhaps right to do so, since the two cultures have so intermixed in Singapore that distinguishing one from another is all but impossible. To confuse the situation further, many Malay/Indonesian restaurants are actually run by Chinese. The most popular dish by far is *satay*, marinated slices of chicken, beef, prawns or mutton, barbecued on a skewer and served with peanut sauce, rice and cucumber.

Occasionally you will find a variation consisting of meat that has been minced and mixed with spices, such as lemon grass, before being shaped and skewered. *Nasi goreng*, originally a breakfast dish, is now a popular and cheap meal for any time of day, consisting of rice fried with chicken or beef, topped with a fried egg and served with prawn crackers (*keropok*). *Nasi padang* is a much more substantial feast of 10 or more small dishes served on individual plates with rice; in some restaurants you select your own dishes from those on display and in others there is a set menu. Other dishes you are likely to encounter include *pepesan* (fish cooked in banana leaves), beef *rendang* cooked in spicy coconut sauce, *ayam goreng* (fried chicken glazed with sweet soy sauce), *sambal udang* (curried prawns), *ikan assam* (fried fish in a tamarind-flavoured curry sauce) and *ikan bilis* (dry-fried whitebait). Traditional accompaniments are *gado-gado*, a salad of raw or lightly steamed vegetables, fried beancurd and peanut sauce, or *tahu goreng*, consisting of bean sprouts mixed with fried beancurd and topped, once again, with peanut sauce.

To sample Malay/Indonesian food, try:

Alkaff Mansion, 10 Telok Blangah Green (tel: 278 6979). Fabulous 1920s mansion filled with period antiques and set in a 47-acre (19ha) hillside park outside the city centre. The speciality is a sumptuous *Rijstaffel* (a spicy, Dutch-influenced Indonesian buffet) but there is also an à la carte menu. The Verandah Bar has superb views over the harbour. *Open*: 12.00–14.30hrs, 19.00–22.30hrs. Expensive.

House of Sundanese, 55 Boat Quay (tel: 534 3775). Good selection of Indonesian specialities, mainly from West Java, including barbecued fish, fried beancurd with vegetable stuffing (*Sedap Ikan Sunda*) and a spicy chicken curry (*Ayam Bumbur Rojak*). The restaurant is sparsely-decorated but this is more than compensated for by the excellence of the food. *Open*: 11.00–14.30hrs, 18.00–22.00hrs. Moderate prices.

Rendezvous Nasi Padang 02–19 Raffles City (tel: 339 7508). Although the premises are new, Rendezvous is a long-established Singaporean institution where you pick and choose from the numerous dishes on display. *Open*: daily, 11.00–21.30hrs. Inexpensive.

Sanur Indonesian, 04–17/18, Centrepoint, 176 Orchard Road (tel: 734 2192). Good Javanese specialities, including *soto madura* (shredded chicken and beansprout soup), *sotong goreng* (deep-fried squid) and *tahu telor* (fried bean curd and eggs served with shredded cucumber and prawn-flavoured sauce). Very busy at lunchtime. *Open*: daily, 11.30–15.15hrs and 18.30–21.30hrs. Inexpensive.

Bintang Timur, 02–08/13 Far East Plaza, 14 Scotts Road (tel: 235 4539). Specialities include beef *satay goreng* (dipped in egg and fried) and *udang goreng lada hitam*, spicy fried prawns. You might also like to try the restaurant's version of fish-head curry – a Singaporean favourite which uses the large and meaty heads of the red snapper fish. *Open*: daily, 11.00–20.00hrs. Moderate prices.

Tambuah Mas Scotts Indonesian Restaurant, 1 Scotts Road 05–14 Shaw Centre (tel: 733 3333). Serves a good variety of Indonesian food. *Open*: daily, 10.00–22.00hrs.

Cantonese Food

Singapore has scores of good Cantonese restaurants and they range from simple and inexpensive eating houses in Chinatown to sophisticated 'new wave' restaurants where top chefs prepare dishes that are a feast for the eye as well as the palate. Many restaurants also serve a special lunchtime menu of *dian xin* (the Mandarin term for *dim sum*), providing an opportunity to taste a large number of savoury dishes without having to spend a fortune.

Among the best of Singapore's Cantonese restaurants are:

Garden Seafood, Goodwood Park Hotel, 22 Scotts Road (tel: 734 7411). Very popular at lunchtime for the wide range of unfailingly good *dian xin*. Other specialities, as the name suggests, include baked crab, steamed prawns and deep-fried cuttlefish stuffed with ham and egg. *Open*: 11.00–14.30hrs and 18.30–23.00hrs. The *dian xin* are inexpensive, but prices generally are on the high side.

Fook Yuen Seafood, 03–05/08 Paragon Shopping Centre, 290 Orchard Road (tel: 235 2211). Another good choice for lunchtime *dian xin*, though the rest of the dishes are not so impressive. *Open*: 11.00–15.00hrs and 18.00–23.00hrs. Moderate to expensive.

Lei Garden, Boulevard Hotel, 200 Orchard Boulevard (tel: 737 2911). Rated one of Singapore's best restaurants, although the exotic ingredients used in many of the dishes means that the bill can mount up rapidly, especially if you go for the dishes based on lobster, shark's fin, bird's nest or abalone. The *dian xin* are highly recommended. *Open*: Monday to Saturday 12.00–15.00hrs, Sunday 11.00–15.00hrs and daily, 18.00–23.00hrs. Expensive.

Tsui Hang Village, 37 Scotts Road (tel: 737 3140). A long-established Singaporean institution popular with family groups and with an expansive menu. The perennially popular house speciality is roast suckling pig – if you want to try it, bear in mind that it is only served at lunchtime. *Open*: 11.30–15.00hrs and 18.00–23.30hrs. Expensive.

Tung Lok Shark's Fin, 04–07/09 Liang Court, 177 River Valley Road (tel: 336 6022). Excellent *dian xin* at lunchtime and a large selection of seafood dishes plus, as the name suggests, shark's fin dishes.

If you have never had it before, superior shark's fin soup, which features on the set menu, is worth trying – even if you end up feeling (as many Westerners do) that the soup would be just as good without the fin! *Open*: 11.30–14.30hrs and 18.30–22.30hrs. Expensive.

Hainanese Food

The classic Hainanese dish is Chicken Rice, a combination of chicken steeped in hot liquid (rather than boiled), splashed with a touch of sesame oil and soy sauce, served with rice cooked in chicken stock and chilli-garlic sauce; Hainanese Chicken Rice is widely available at Hawker Centres.

The Hainanese also serve the popular Steamboat, where a chafing dish of stock is placed in the centre of the table so that diners can cook their own meat, seafood and vegetables, dipping them into various accompanying sauces.

Charming Garden, Novotel Orchid, 214 Dunearn Road, (tel: 250 3322). A good place to try Hainanese specialities as well as standards such as Chicken Rice and Steamboat. *Open*: 12.00–14.30hrs, 18.00–22.30hrs. Moderate to expensive.

Herbal Chinese Food

Traditionally, Chinese food is categorised according to the balance of Yin and Yang in the ingredients. In herbal food, this balance is carefully calculated and menus are also chosen according to what ails you at the time, with a herbal specialist recommending the appropriate remedy.

Imperial Herbal Restaurant, Metropole Hotel, 41 Seah Street, (tel: 337 0491). The most famous herbal restaurant in Singapore, with a resident herbalist. You might not fancy the scorpions on prawn toast (a nerve tonic) but there are other tempting dishes which are not only good for you but taste good too. *Open*: 11.30–14.00hrs, 18.30–22.00hrs. Expensive.

Hokkien Food

Hokkien people form the biggest ethnic Chinese group in Singapore and much of the island's hawker food is based on Hokkien cuisine; indeed, the ubiquitous Singapore fried noodles is essentially a version of Hokkien Fried Mee, a dish of thick noodles fried with seafood, pork and vegetables. There are, however, several sophisticated restaurants serving Hokkien food, which tends to be richer and more substantial than Cantonese; typical dishes are *poh piah*, (soft-skinned spring rolls filled with cabbage, prawns, sausage and egg), *oh chien* (oyster omelette) and *khong bak* (belly pork in a steamed wheat bun). Try Hokkien food at:

Beng Hiang, 112, Amoy Street, (tel: 221 6684). Hokkien specialities plus excellent suckling pig and fried squid balls. *Open*: daily, 11.30–14.00hrs and 18.00–21.00hrs. Moderate prices.

Beng Thin Hoon Kee, 05–02, OCBC Building, 55 Chuliah Street (tel: 533 7708). A Singaporean institution going back to 1948. Excellent duck and pork dishes. No credit cards. *Open*: daily, 11.00–15.00hrs and 18.00–22.00hrs.

Peking Food

Peking duck is now famous worldwide and there are plenty of opportunities to enjoy this dish of crispy duck skin eaten with spring onions and cucumbers wrapped in a pancake and dipped in plum sauce – virtually every Chinese restaurant in Singapore features Peking duck, even if they specialise in other regional Chinese cuisines. You will also find lamb on the menu of Peking-style restaurants, as well as freshwater fish such as tench, usually baked in a sweet vinegar sauce. Instead of rice, it is traditional to eat steamed bread or noodles with northern Chinese dishes.

Try Peking cuisine at:

Prima Tower Revolving Restaurant, 201 Keppel Road (tel: 272 8822). Locals claim the Peking duck served here is the best in town and the restaurant itself, located at the top of the harbour-side tower, offers superb views. *Open*: daily, 11.00–15.00hrs and 19.00–22.30hrs. Expensive.

Pine Court, Mandarin Hotel, 333 Orchard Road (tel: 737 4411). Peking duck, baked tench and marinated lamb served in a palatial restaurant with fine views. In addition, there is a popular and inexpensive buffet lunch which features a very wide range of regional dishes and provides an excellent introduction to Chinese cuisine. *Open*: daily, 12.00–14.30hrs and 19.00–22.30hrs. Moderate to expensive.

Szechuan Food
Singaporeans like their food spicy and Szechuan food, with its liberal use of fiery red chilli peppers, is very popular. There are, of course, many less fiery dishes for those who have not developed a tolerance for chilli, including duck smoked over a mixture of camphor wood chips and jasmine tea leaves.
Try Szechuan food at:
Dragon City, Novotel Orchid Inn, 214 Dunearn Road (tel: 254 7070). The best Szechuan restaurant in Singapore, according to local *aficionados*. The extensive menu runs the whole gamut of this cuisine from luxurious dishes such as lobster fried with chilli to humbler eel, aubergine and beancurd preparations. *Open*: daily, 11.30–14.30hrs and 18.30–22.30hrs. Moderate to expensive.
Golden Phoenix, Equatorial Hotel, 429 Bukit Timah Road (tel: 732 0431). This long-established restaurant led the field until the chef moved to the Dragon City and still satisfies a discerning clientele. The garlic prawns are rated highly, and the camphor and tea smoked duck is served Peking-duck style, with pancakes and spring onions. *Open*: daily, 12.00–15.00hrs and 18.30–23.00hrs. Moderate to expensive.
Min Jiang, Goodwood Park Hotel, 22 Scotts Road (tel: 737 7411). Excellent chilli prawns, smoked duck, eel and Szechuan hot and sour soup. *Open*: daily, 12.00–14.30hrs and 18.30–22.30hrs. Moderate prices.

Seafood Restaurants
Old traditions die hard, and Singapore people like to drive to the coast for a seafood meal,

even though the food they consume may very well have been flown in from China or Australia or trucked across the causeway from Malaysia. Most fish is now purchased at the big central market in industrial Jurong. Even so, the fish is as fresh as it could be, since a key feature of many seafood restaurants is the long wall of tanks displaying an array of colourful crustaceans, kept alive until some customer points a fateful finger and orders a dish of chilli crab or steamed prawns.

Local seafood cuisine is based on Chinese cooking methods – steaming, stir-frying and deep frying – and liberal use is made of chilli and garlic. The number one seafood dish, without which many local people would consider a meal incomplete, is chilli crab – fresh crabs, stir-fried with garlic, chilli, tomato sauce and egg. It is a messy and difficult dish to eat, requiring patience and skill to extract the

Seafood under the stars: the city's eateries offer a feast for all the senses

It tastes as good as it looks!

juicy morsels of meat from the shell, and locals argue endlessly over which part of the crab has the most flavour.

Seafood restaurants can be very utilitarian – eating with your fingers at rough tables under a tarpaulin or tin roof does, however, seem to make the food taste that bit fresher.

Good seafood restaurants include:

Long Beach Seafood, 1018 Leisure Court, East Coast Park (tel: 445 8833). Choose between eating al fresco or in the dining section indoors. It is safe to trust the recommendations of the chef, as relayed by the waiter, and wait and see what turns up. Black pepper crab, the house speciality, is too peppery for some tastes but the squid dishes are highly recommended. *Open*: daily, 17.00–00.30hrs. Expensive to moderate prices.

Palm Beach Seafood, 5 Stadium Walk, Leisure Park (tel: 344 3088). Huge and popular restaurant seating nearly 600 when full (which it often is at weekends). There are no menus, so ask for guidance and if in doubt go for chilli crab, prawns in black bean sauce and *yu cha kuay* – seafood stuffed steamed buns. *Open*: daily, 17.30hrs–midnight. Moderate prices.

Sentosa Riverboat Restaurant, 1 Garden Avenue, Sentosa (tel: 275 0176). Three-storey restaurant in a turn-of-the-century Mississippi Riverboat moored next to the ferry terminal. The best location is the seafood restaurant on the upper deck, with panoramic views over the city skyline. *Open*: 10.00–22.00hrs. Expensive.

Singa Inn Seafood Restaurant, 920 East Coast Parkway (tel: 345 1111). One of the biggest outdoor seafood restaurants on the coast. Catch your own live lobster, crabs, fish and prawns from their tanks and order them any way you want – steamed, barbecued, or in a sauce. Good chilli crab and seafood vegetable soup, and good value set menu meals for two people. *Open*: 18.00–23.00hrs. Moderate to expensive.

Indian Food

The curry houses of Little India serve food as cheap as you will find in Singapore, principally vegetable dishes with rice, served up on a banana leaf. Be prepared to eat these dishes in the traditional southern Indian manner, using the fingers of the right hand (spoons and forks will be provided, however, if you ask). These dishes are often quite fiery and you will probably want a glass of yoghurt by your side to cool and clear your palate.

If you do not want to rough it, there are plenty of more refined Indian restaurants serving northern Indian dishes and excellent tandooris.

Annalakshmi, 02–10 Excelsior Hotel and Shopping Centre, 5 Coleman Street (tel: 339 9993). This restaurant, run to raise money for Indian charities by using volunteer cooks and waiting staff, is the best place to discover the sheer variety of Indian vegetarian cuisine from North and South India. The extensive lunchtime buffet is a revelation and the combination of friendly, helpful staff and attractive modern and antique Indian furnishings (some of which are for sale) makes eating here a pleasurable adventure. As well as various food dishes the restaurant also serves speciality drinks such as: Mango Tharang, a mixture of mango juice, honey and ginger. *Open*: daily, 11.30–15.30hrs and 19.00–22.00hrs. Moderate prices.

Banana Leaf Apollo, 56 Race Course Road (tel: 293 8682). This restaurant is a bit like an up-market canteen, with rows of long tables which you share with all-comers. Your 'plate' is a washed banana leaf which will be placed in front of you as soon as you are seated and piled with rice and vegetables. You select your main course from the dishes displayed at the counter – fish-head curry is the speciality and the choice includes crabs, tiger prawns, tandoori chicken and mutton masala. *Open*: daily, 10.30–22.00hrs. Moderate prices.

Kinara North Indian Shore Cuisine, 57 Boat Quay (tel: 533 0412). Riverside restaurant specialising in Punjabi dishes, including aromatic curries, Tandoori chicken and desserts such as kulfi. *Open*: 11.30–14.30hrs, 18.30– 22.30hrs. Moderate prices.

Komala Vilas, 76 Serangoon Road (tel: 293 6980). Authentic Little India café-style restaurant serving the local population with vegetarian curries and a choice of rice or pancakes. *Open*: daily, 06.00–22.00hrs. Inexpensive.

Tandoor, Holiday Inn Park View, 11 Cavenagh Road (tel: 733 8333). Upmarket restaurant designed to make you feel like a maharajah, with live traditional Indian music at dinner. Excellent seafood dishes are served, such as lobster *nisha*, and crab *goa* in addition to all the classic tandoori dishes. *Open*: daily, 12.00–15.00hrs and 19.00–23.00hrs. Expensive.

Thai Food
The spiciness of Thai food appeals to the Singaporean palate and there are several good restaurants staffed by Thai chefs to choose from:
Thanying Restaurant, 2nd floor, Amara Hotel, 165 Tanjong Pagar Road (tel: 224 4488). Good Thai cuisine is available at this hotel restaurant.

Japanese Food
The cost of flying in absolutely fresh raw ingredients and of employing skilled Japanese chefs means that Singapore's Japanese restaurants are not cheap and yet they are flourishing – thanks, in part, to the large number of Japanese tourists who visit Singapore, and to the fact that young Singaporeans look to Japan as the arbiter of everything that is currently stylish and chic in Asia.
Kurumaya, Dai-Ichi Hotel, 81 Anson Road (tel: 224 1133). As you would expect, this Japanese-owned hotel has one of the best Japanese restaurants in Singapore, though to see the resident chef convert live lobster into *sashimi* is not an experience for the squeamish. Excellent *tempura* and *teppanyaki*. *Open*: daily, 12.00–14.30hrs and 18.30–22.30hrs. Expensive.
Suntory, 06–01 Delfi Orchard, 402 Orchard Road (tel: 732 5111). Arguably the best Japanese restaurant in Singapore with separate dining rooms for *tempura*, *sushi*, *shabu-shabu* and *teppanyaki*, where you can watch the chefs at work. Special *teppanyaki* is highly recommended, as are the inexpensive set lunches, consisting of beautifully light *tempura*, rice, soup and pickles. *Open*: daily, 12.00–15.00hrs and 18.30–23.00hrs. Prices range from inexpensive to very expensive.

Western Food
It might seem perverse to eat Western food in Asia, were it not for the fact that Singapore has some top-class 'international' restaurants serving dishes that combine the freshest local ingredients – especially seafood – cooked with flair, often by highly skilled French, Swiss or Austrian chefs. Among the best are:
Al Forno Trattoria, 275 Thomson Road, 01–07 (tel: 256 2848). *Open*: 12.00–14.00hrs and 18.30–22.30hrs.
Casablanca, 7 Emerald Hill Road (tel: 235 9328). Characterful bistro-style restaurant set in a converted Straits-Chinese house, and serving wholesome unpretentious French-style food. The house speciality, rock-fish soup, is well worth trying. *Open*: daily, 12.00–15.00hrs and 19.00hrs–midnight. Moderate to expensive.
Chico's n Charlies, 05–01 Liat Towers, 541 Orchard Road (tel: 734 1753). Lively and informal Mexican restaurant, a fun place to eat serving all the standard

Cooking a suckling pig on charcoal

Mexican dishes. *Open*: daily, 11.00–23.00hrs. Moderate prices.

Gordon Grill, Goodwood Park Hotel, 22 Scotts Road (tel: 737 7411). Tartan-clad waiters and Scottish inspiration – Scotch salmon, Angus beef and haggis, plus a wide selection of single malt whiskies. *Open*: daily, 12.00–14.30hrs and 19.00–23.00hrs. Expensive.

Harbour Grill, Hilton International Hotel, 581 Orchard Road (tel: 737 2233). Adventurous cooking, always superb and popular with businessmen and well-heeled gourmets. The five-course Surprise Gourmet Dinner changes daily and is well worth sampling – the surprise is that the content of each dish is only revealed when it is placed before you. *Open*: Monday to Friday 12.00–15.00hrs and daily, 19.00–23.00hrs. Expensive.

Mövenpick, 39 Boat Quay, (tel: 538 8200). Swiss restaurant specialising in steak tartare (12 different versions), raclette, tender veal Zurichoise and, of course, a good range of Swiss cheeses. *Open*: Sunday to Thursday 11.00hrs–midnight, Friday and Saturday 11.00–01.00hrs. Inexpensive set lunches and dinners, otherwise prices are moderate to expensive.

Nutmegs, Hyatt Regency Hotel, 10–12 Scotts Road (tel: 738 1234). Californian-style dishes such as crab coleslaw, pasta with scallops and pistachio sauce and prawns on potato risotto are on the menu here. *Open*: daily, 12.00–14.30hrs and 19.00–23.00hrs. Expensive.

Pasta Fresca Da Salvatore, 30 Boat Quay (tel: 532 6283). Popular Italian restaurant with a relaxed atmosphere and good food at affordable prices. The usual pasta dishes are complemented by Italian sandwiches known as Puccia (a flat loaf stuffed with anything from ham, mushrooms and artichokes to cheese and tomatoes). *Open*: 24 hours. Moderate.

Prego, Westin Plaza Hotel, 2 Stamford Road (tel: 431 5156). Excellent restaurant serving everything from pizza and pasta meals to classic Italian dishes. *Open*: 12.00–14.30hrs and 18.30–22.30hrs. Moderate to expensive.

Sizzling Rock Speciality Restaurant, 51 and 51A Boat Quay (tel: 538 6851). Unusual restaurant with a 'prehistoric' theme, decorated with cave drawings. Customers cook their own food on pre-heated granite slabs, which stay hot for about an hour. A choice of meat, poultry and seafood with several sauces is on offer. *Open*: 12.00–14.30hrs, 18.00– 22.30hrs. Moderate prices.

TGI Friday's, 9 Penang Road, 01–24 The Glass House Parkmall (tel: 334 7811). The ambience of this lively, atmospheric restaurant is part of the attraction but the food is also good, with an extensive menu which includes steaks, ribs, hamburgers, seafood, pasta and pizza. Popular choices include deep fried chicken wings, chicken fajitas, and full-slab ribs. *Open*: Sunday to Thursday 11.30hrs–midnight, Friday to Saturday 11.30–01.00hrs. Moderate prices.

Hawker Food

Once upon a time, the streets of Singapore were lively with food hawkers who would set up their stalls at busy corners and shout their wares to passers-by. The Government then decided that hawkers were a nuisance, a traffic hazard, probably unhygienic and a force for disorder.

Fortunately, instead of wiping hawkers off the face of Singapore, the Singaporean authorities encouraged them to set up permanent stalls in large, purpose-built food centres, where standards of cleanliness could be supervised. Thus was born a unique Singapore phenomenon.

Eating out at hawker food stalls is an experience every visitor should try at least once – and if you are on a tight budget, you can eat here regularly, feasting on an extraordinary range of offerings for a few dollars a head.

To a first-time visitor, the lack of menus and unfamiliarity of the food on display may be rather intimidating. The secret is to ask what each dish is – and be brave, don't just settle for the familiar noodles or chicken with rice or you will miss all the pleasure of extending your culinary repertoire. The dishes are cheap enough, after all, for it not to matter if you decide to leave a dish that you do not like too much.

Arriving at a hawker centre, wander round and look at all the stalls to gain an idea of the different types of food on offer. You can order food from as many different stalls as you wish; just tell the stallholder your table number or, if it doesn't have a number, point to where you intend to sit.

Some stalls specialise in one type of food – *satay*, for example, or noodles or freshly squeezed fruit juices. Others offer a wider variety of snacks. Stallholders are generally friendly and speak English, so take your time and ask questions if in doubt.

The most central hawker food stalls are located at:

Newton Circus, junction of Scotts, Bukit, Timah and Newton roads, a short walk from Orchard Road. The fact that many tourists come here is an advantage if you are at all hesitant – the stallholders are well used to helping first-time visitors. *Open*: 18.00hrs–midnight or later.

Chinatown Complex, Smith Street. All kinds of regional Chinese foods can be sampled at this hawker centre, at a fraction of the price you would pay in a restaurant. *Open*: 08.00hrs–midnight.

Lau Pa Sat Festival Market, 18 Raffles Quay. Beautifully restored Victorian ironwork market, with craft stalls as well as hawker stands.

Picnic Food Court, Scotts Shopping Centre basement, Scotts Road. More upmarket version of a hawker centre, with air-conditioning. *Open*: 10.00–22.00hrs.

Lagoon Food Centre, East Coast Parkway. Lively centre serving the local population and reputed to have the best *satay* in Singapore. *Open*: 11.00hrs–midnight or later.

SHOPPING

Singapore promotes itself as the shopping capital of the world. This claim is justified principally by the sheer number of stores selling everything from sandalwood fans and ginseng to the latest video cameras and designer fashions. Added to that is the sheer convenience of being able to find everything you could want to buy, all laid out in air-conditioned plazas that are open every day from morning until late at night. Specialist shops sell the very latest models and if they do not happen to stock a particular make or model they will get it for you within an hour from the wholesaler or another branch. Staff tend to be less aggressive than their Hong Kong counterparts and are usually helpful or friendly – if not, you can always go elsewhere.

Prices

Singapore also claims to be a very cheap place to shop. Whether that still holds true depends on a number of factors. Historically, prices have been low because few goods attract import duty and there was no purchase tax or VAT. However, a 3 per cent Goods and Service Tax was introduced by the Government on 1 April 1994 (visitors can reclaim this on purchases over S$500 at Changi Airport) which will increase prices; shop rents and salaries have also risen and, although bargaining is still the norm in many stores, retailers are more protective of their margins than they used to be. They are more likely to resort to other practices to attract custom. Computer sellers will, for example, load free software into your lap-top computer or AppleMac as an inducement to buy.

Exchange rates are another factor to bear in mind. The Singapore dollar is a strong and stable currency. If the currency you hold happens to be in the doldrums, think carefully before you part with your money. It may well be possible to find electronic goods being sold just as cheaply in discount stores back home.

Finally, bear in mind that you may have to pay duty and tax when you import your purchases back home. Duty-free limits are very easy to exceed, so do be aware of what yours are.

Rip-offs

Try as they might, the Singapore authorities have not stamped out all sharp practices. There are plenty of so-called 'copy watches', counterfeit Rolex watches and Dior handbags, masquerading as the genuine article. Beware of anyone who offers temptingly low prices compared to other retailers – the goods may not be all they seem (on the other hand, if you insist on buying a fake Rolex, bargain hard and expect rock-bottom prices). When you buy, ensure that the price includes all the accessories. It has been known for retailers to charge extra for attachments that are actually integral to the product. Check that electrical goods are compatible with standards back home (UK, New Zealand and

Australia: 220–240 volts, 50 cycles; USA and Canada: 110–120 volts, 60 cycles). Be sure to check the warranty terms before you part with money, and ensure that the product serial numbers and those on the warranty are the same.
Worldwide warranties are only issued by authorised dealers. Some retailers sell what are known as 'parallel imports'; these usually have very restricted warranties, valid only in the country from which the goods were imported. Parallel imports are cheaper, but bear in mind that the cost of repairs could wipe out the value of any savings you make on the purchase price.
Make sure that everything you buy is in working order and watch it being packed so that no items are 'inadvertently' missed out. Finally, be sure to get a written itemised receipt. You will need this in case of problems later, for insurance purposes and for customs inspection back home. A cash register slip is simply not adequate.
You can avoid problems by shopping with members of the Good Retailers Scheme. The tourist office produce *A Guide to Shopping*, there is also the *Official Shopping Directory* published by CASE. Members display a red Merlion sticker (the symbol of Singapore). The scheme is strictly controlled to ensure that members do not sell pirated, counterfeit or defective goods. If you need to seek redress, contact the Singapore Tourist Promotion Board (tel: 736 6622) or the Consumers' Association of Singapore (CASE) (tel: 270 4611). If necessary, you can also seek compensation through the Small Claims Tribunal (see **Complaints** in the **Directory** section).

Bargaining
Many retailers in Singapore work on the principle of low margins and high turnover – another reason why prices here can be low. How low depends on your skill at bargaining (and the mood of the shopkeeper!).
Do your homework first by visiting shops to compare prices (some free shopping guides available in hotels helpfully list the manufacturer's recommended retail price for many popular items). In smaller shops you will be greeted by keen salesmen when you enter and will be subjected to high-pressure sales techniques, so be prepared to fend them off until you find a shop where you feel comfortable with the sales staff and prices.
Bargaining is a game with a purpose, which both sides should enjoy. Shop assistants are good at sensing your mood and intentions, and if they sniff a potential sale they will try and keep you in the shop until you have been won over. You must be equally subtle, knowing at what point to withdraw your interest and using such phrases as: 'I still can't afford that price... maybe I can find it cheaper elsewhere'. As a final tactic to drive the price down, you can always head for the door. Best prices are given to those who play their part with skill and humour, not to those who bully

and expect unreasonable discounts. Remember, too, that you are under a moral obligation to go ahead with the purchase once you have agreed on a price. If you do not enjoy the game, shop at department stores where the prices are fixed and fair.

Credit Cards
In shops where bargaining is the norm, lowest prices are reserved for customers paying with cash or travellers' cheques. Tell the vendor if you intend to pay by credit card as he needs to make allowances for the card company's commission. This is not the same as imposing a surcharge for credit card use, a practice that the card companies frown upon. If it happens to you, insist that the surcharge is shown as a separate item on the receipt. Forward this evidence to the card company which will take corrective action and refund the surcharge. American Express, Carte Blanche, Diners, MasterCard and Visa are accepted by almost all stores.

Do Not Buy
You will still find goods made from the by-products of endangered species on sale in Singapore. This trade is illegal and puts you at the risk of prosecution if you try to export or import prohibited goods. The same is true of ivory, though special arrangements can be made for certified antiques.

Shopping Hours
It seems that Singapore's shops never close. Most are open daily, 10.00–21.00hrs or later.

A traditional medical hall in Chinatown can offer cures for many ailments

Tangs department store and some up-market boutiques close on Sundays.

Tailoring
The clothes sold in Singapore tend to be on the small side and some visitors may find difficulty in buying clothes that fit off the peg. Help is at hand in the form of numerous tailors and dressmakers. Most textile stores offer a make-up service and the workmanship is of a high standard. You can have existing clothes copied or choose your design from pattern books. Do not expect miracles; good

clothes cannot be made overnight and you should allow at least two days for the garments to be completed and set aside time to attend fitting sessions. Some tailors do offer a 24-hour service but they will charge a premium and there will not be time for subtle adjustments. Prices are reasonable; you pay a tailoring charge on top of the material cost and the combined cost is usually cheaper than the price of an off-the-peg garment made of the same materials.

Delivery and Shipping

Many shops will deliver goods to your hotel for a small charge. Department stores will deliver for free if you spend over a certain amount and arrange shipping. You do, however, run the slight risk that objects go missing or get damaged in transit. Check insurance coverage when having goods shipped home.

Where to Shop

Department stores

Dip your toes in the water by visiting one of the major department stores in the Orchard Road area. Here the prices are fixed and there is no pressure to buy (indeed, getting served can sometimes be difficult!) so you can happily browse and compare prices. Metro, DFS and Tangs (known as the 'Harrods' of Singapore) are 'home grown' stores selling local and imported goods and fashions. Try Daimaru, Sogo and Yaohan for all things Japanese and Isetan for smart Japanese fashions. Galeries Lafayette specialises in French *haute couture*, jewellery and accessories. British and European imports are sold at the long-established Robinson's and at St Michael (the Singapore arm of Marks & Spencer).

Orchard Road

Orchard Road, once a nutmeg plantation, is now synonymous with shopping. This wide boulevard, over 1½ miles (2.5km) in length, is lined with multi-storey plazas selling everything that the world has to offer. You will find it confusing at first – everybody does – but if you enjoy shopping you will love the fact that every turning brings a new surprise. Having said that, you will not miss much if you only sample one or two shopping centres; most are clones of each other and many retailers have branches in every shopping centre.

To make sense of the maze, arm yourself with one of the shopping guides available free at every hotel. The *American Express Map of Singapore* is the simplest and most portable. The most rewarding stretch of Orchard Road starts at Centrepoint (near Somerset MRT station) and extends up to the junction with Tanglin Road. Centrepoint itself is home to Robinson's and St Michael, and has a useful supermarket and pharmacy in its basement (called Cold Storage) and two large bookshops, Times and MPH, facing each other across the top floor and selling a wide range of English-language books and newspapers.

Right next door, by way of complete contrast, is Cuppage Terrace, a row of old and ornate shop-houses. Look for No 31, BabaZar, where you can browse amongst ancient and modern Asian handicrafts – everything from carved wood doors and shadow puppets to inexpensive toys. Several more gaily painted Straits-Chinese shop-houses line Peranakan Place, the other side of Centrepoint, a good place to rest over coffee and cakes at the Emerald Mall Sidewalk Café or the Café d'Orient. Further up Orchard Road is another exercise in contrasts. At the Rolex centre, on the ground floor of the Tong building, you can part with more than most of us earn in a year for a genuine Rolex watch. In next-door Lucky Plaza you are quite likely to be approached by a tout offering you a low-priced imitation. Alternatively, go and browse among the antique watches sold at Good Old Days (Lucky Plaza 4th Floor).

Lucky Plaza has all the atmosphere of a bazaar and, besides watches, you will find scores of shops specialising in cameras, video and stereo systems, and leather goods. Competition is fierce and you can expect to be approached by touts employed to attract you into their store with promises of the cheapest prices in town. Do

Pick your plaza in Orchard Road

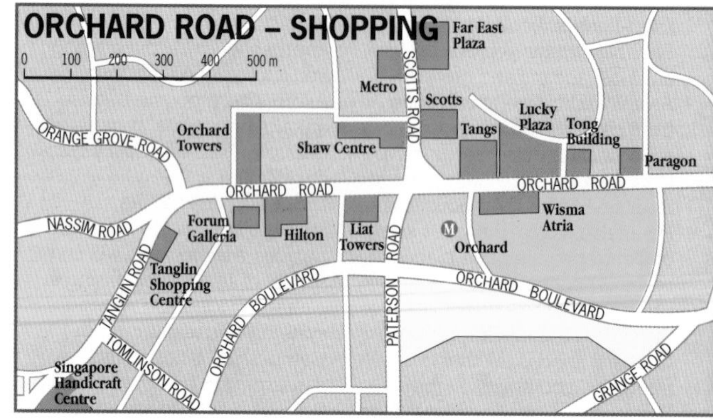

not believe them; somebody has to pay their commission and, besides, touting is illegal. You should be suspicious of any shop that resorts to such practices. If the hard-sell approach gets too much, cross the road to the quiet sophistication of Wisma Atria, lined with the boutiques of exclusive – and expensive – couturiers and perfumiers. There is no bargaining here and, as the saying goes, if you have to ask the price you probably cannot afford it. Orchard Road gets more up-market from here on, with galleries devoted to the sale of classy designer wear, jewellery and accessories, plus antiques and furnishings in the Hilton Shopping Gallery. After Tangs, considered the best department store in Singapore (but strongly rivalled by Japanese newcomers like Sogo), you can divert into Scotts Road. Here you will find the vast Far East Plaza, with over 800 stores and the Shaw Centre, a lively place where you are more likely to find cheaper clothes and gifts. For more goods that don't cost a lifetime's savings, continue up Orchard Road and turn left into Tanglin Road. At No 1 you will find Jim Thompson's Thai Silk Shop selling beautiful and affordable silks on the ground floor (everything from simple headscarves to full evening wear) and Indonesian *ikat* wall hangings above.

Next comes Tanglin Shopping Centre, the place to come for antiques, furnishings and fabrics, carpets and tailors. Absorbing shops include Design Thai (in the basement) selling colourful fabrics, the China Silk House and Hassan's Carpets. For old books and prints visit Antiques of the Orient and for a good range of travel and history books covering Southeast Asia go to Select Books.

Browse through the many antique shops here but be careful; prices are very high and even experts can make mistakes. You will not be very happy if you later discover that you could have bought something similar at auction back home for a fraction of the price. Fortunately many of

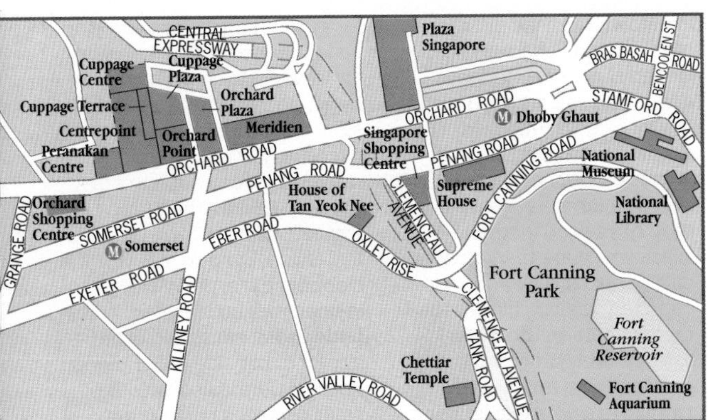

the shops in Tanglin Shopping Centre also sell quality reproductions at much more affordable prices.

Just beyond Tanglin Shopping Centre lies Tudor Court, all English-style timber and gables, a characterful outpost of the Orchard Road shopping district that has been colonised, once again, by designer-clothes boutiques.

Off Orchard Road

A comprehensive tour of Orchard Road only scratches the surface of Singapore's shopping opportunities. Local people, who flock to the latest and biggest, crowd Marina Square at weekends, currently the largest shopping centre in Singapore, and then go on to Raffles City, with its big Sogo department store and well-stocked Kinokuniya bookshop. If you are short of time, or hate shopping but want to get a feel for what makes Singapore hum, go to one of these two centres.

The People's Park Complex, adjacent to Chinatown, lacks the flashiness of its downtown rivals but is the place to go to drive a hard bargain if you are interested in buying electronic goods. Computer freaks will find everything they could ask for at the Funan Centre, 109 North Bridge Road, and still more electronic goods at keen prices will be found at the Sim Lim Square complex, 1 Rochor Canal Road.

Local flavour

Singapore has always been a bridge between East and West. As early as 1511 a Portuguese explorer described the island as a 'world fair'. Today the shops selling Italian fashions and Japanese technology shout the loudest but you can also find much that is peculiarly Asian. Singapore itself does not have much in the way of indigenous crafts but it compensates by importing and selling everything from baskets woven in the jungles of Borneo to statues sculpted in jade. Seeking them out will take you to some of the more traditional parts of Singapore.

Chinatown Here the old shop-houses of traditional herbalists, wooden shoemakers, clog carvers and calligraphers stand side-by-side with modern complexes stocked with jade, ceramics, *cloisonné,* textiles and lacquered furniture. For really cheap buys head for the Chinatown centre market, down Smith Street off New Bridge Road. Here, among the wizened grandmothers selling water chestnuts and garlic, you can buy everything from a rice-straw hat to a cigarette lighter shaped like a video camera – something to take home if you cannot afford the real thing. Jewellery shops in the South Bridge Centre glitter with the bright reflections of very pure (24 carat) yellow Chinese gold. Prices here reflect the current gold price. Jewellery is sold by weight, and then you bargain over the premium that you pay for the workmanship. If you fall on hard times you can trade your jewellery in again for cash, or even make a profit if the price of gold has risen in the interim. Stores in South Bridge Road also specialise in jade, a stone highly prized by the Chinese who prefer the more expensive darker colours to the paler Nephrite or brighter Jadeite. Inexpensive earrings and pendants make good presents but only buy from reputable dealers and seek expert advice before paying high prices for antique jade and sculptures; fakes and artificial jade are commonplace.

Arab Street, off Beach Road, is not the bargain basement it once was. Locals blame tourists for pushing up the prices – it is no longer possible to bargain and jewellers' shops have begun to take the place of stores that used to sell a miscellany of goods, from prayer rugs and copies of the *Koran* to baskets, hats and furniture of rice-straw, bamboo and rattan. Even so, it is worth stopping by, especially for leatherwork and textiles.

Little India, consisting of the streets either side of Serangoon Road, is permeated with the smell of spices being ground and the shops are crowded with richly coloured fabrics, embroidered blouses, silk saris and handwoven cottons, brassware, sandalwood and handmade jewellery. Prices are keen and sideshows abound, from fortune tellers to garland makers who will sell you a necklace of fragrant jasmine.

Out of town

Holland Village, off Holland Road, used to be an expatriate enclave and expats still come here to shop because the stores are geared to Western tastes and the prices are cheaper than in Orchard Road. Alternatively, take a taxi to Parkway Parade and see where many Singaporeans prefer to shop – the prices are keener and you can sustain your energy by eating at the hawker food stalls.

Last gasp

For last-minute buys, don't forget Changi Airport. Terminal 1 has around a dozen shops, Terminal 2 has 30 or more. The emphasis tends to be more on luxury goods than cheap souvenirs.

ACCOMMODATION

Singapore's hotel industry is a perfect illustration of the economic law of supply and demand. Every five years or so there is a wave of new hotel building followed by a glut of cheap rooms. Occupancy rates then creep up to the point where hoteliers can charge top prices and be confident of filling their rooms year round, helped by the buoyant conference industry. Then a new round of hotel building begins.

Just at the moment, prices are relatively stable. With most major new hotel projects now completed and occupancy rates remaining relatively high it's unlikely that the bargain room rates of the past will be repeated.

The cheapest rooms are likely to cost around S$175 (inclusive of taxes) but more typically you can expect to pay a minimum of S$250 for a single room, about S$300 for a double, and S$450 upwards for deluxe rooms or suites.

Some of the best deals are to be had by booking an inclusive flight and accommodation package to Singapore, since tour operators are able to bulk buy hotel rooms at much cheaper rates than any individual can. Alternatively, you can wait until you arrive and book at the airport hotel-reservations counter, traditionally the best place to find cheap deals at short notice. Even so, you may find your choice of hotel restricted, especially during the peak winter visitor season. As a general rule, hotels that are located away from the Orchard Road area tend to be cheaper; depending on the time of year, you may well find that you can make considerable savings by choosing a hotel that does not have an Orchard or Scotts Road address – more than enough to compensate for the additional cost of taxis to and from the centre.

Marina Square hotels...

Since nearly all Singapore's hotels have been built within the last 15 years or so, they tend to be all of a type, with little to distinguish one from another in architectural terms. With the exception of Raffles and the Goodwood Park Hotel, you should not expect old-world charm or ambience, but you will find that service standards are excellent, and that rooms are

...offer rooms with a bay view

clean, modern and comfortably furnished. Air-conditioning is standard and you can usually count on 24-hour room service, a TV, radio, mini-bar, International Direct Dial telephone and a good-sized bathroom. Virtually every hotel has a travel desk where bookings can be made for tours, restaurants or entertainment, as well as a newskiosk/drugstore, beauty salon/hairdresser, a coffee shop, bar and choice of restaurants.

Hotels

Allson, 101 Victoria Street (tel: 336 0811). Two blocks from Raffles City, shuttle bus service to Orchard Road. 412 rooms and good Szechuan restaurant. Moderate prices.

Amara Hotel, 165 Tanjong Pagar Road (tel: 224 4488). Moderately priced, 330-room hotel. Chinese and Western restaurants, adjacent to Chinatown.

ANA, 16 Nassim Hill (tel: 732 1222). Just off Tanglin Road, well-run hotel with 450 rooms and no-smoking floors, business and fitness centres. Expensive.

Apollo Hotel, 405 Havelock Road (tel: 733 2081). 300-room hotel, moderate prices, with Japanese, Indonesian and Chinese restaurants. No-smoking floors.

Bencoolen, 47 Bencoolen Street (tel: 336 0822). One of Singapore's cheapest, 69 rooms.

Boulevard, 200 Orchard Boulevard (tel: 737 2911). Over 500 rooms, used by tour groups, but with good coffee-shop and American, Japanese, Chinese and Indian restaurants. Moderate prices.

Carlton, 76 Bras Basah Road (tel: 338 8333). 400-room hotel with no-smoking floors, fitness and business centres. Moderate prices, discounts available.

Crown Prince, 270 Orchard Road (tel: 732 1111). Right in the centre of the Orchard Road shopping run, 300 rooms, no-smoking floors and free in-house video movies. Highly regarded *sushi* restaurant, plus Western and Szechuan food. Moderate prices.

Dynasty, 320 Orchard Road (tel: 734 9900). Next to Tangs on the Scotts and Orchard Road junction, a busy 400-room hotel with no-smoking floors and good restaurants serving Western and Chinese food. Competitive prices for such a central location.

Excelsior, 5 Coleman Street (tel: 338 7733). Pleasant location just off the colonial district. Good service and extra touches like coffee- and tea-making facilities in all of the 300 rooms. Moderate prices.

Garden (Best Western), 14 Balmoral Road (tel: 235 3344). Pleasant 200-room hotel in a quiet district, with swimming pool, gym and sauna, five minutes' taxi ride from Orchard Road. Its non-central location keeps prices moderate.

Goodwood Park, 22 Scotts Road (tel: 737 7411). This luxurious hotel was built in 1900 as the Teutonia Club by German expatriates in the style of a Rhineland Castle and it rivalled the more famous Raffles hotel in the 1930s, when famous guests included the Duke of Windsor. The hotel was beautifully restored in 1978 by the Singaporean businessman, Khoo Teck Puat, and the many original furnishings and paintings contribute to the atmosphere of elegance and grandeur. Half of the 200 rooms consist of large and airy suites, and there are numerous relaxing corners where you can take high tea overlooking the cloistered gardens. The Scottish-inspired Gordon Grill is popular with expatriate Europeans for business entertainment, and there are good Chinese and Japanese restaurants as well. Expensive.

Grand Central, 22 Cavenagh Road (tel: 737 9944). One block north of Orchard Road and with everything you could want from a central hotel, including Japanese and Chinese restaurants. 400 rooms at moderate prices.

Harbour View Dai-Ichi, 81 Anson Road (tel: 224 1133). Aimed at Japanese travellers and those visiting Shenton Way's business and financial district. 400 rooms, including Japanese-style *tatami* rooms, business centre and first-class cuisine. Moderate prices.

Hilton International Singapore, 581 Orchard Road (tel: 737 2233). A luxurious hotel where the service is impeccable, especially if you choose one of the top-floor suites designed by Givenchy, complete with jacuzzi and balconies large enough to host a dinner party. Excellent business facilities plus swimming pool, gym and sauna and an arcade of exclusive designer-name boutiques. The Harbour Grill restaurant attracts top people and the Inn of Happiness on the top floor serves some of Singapore's best Chinese food. 400 rooms. Expensive.

Dynasty Hotel – a modern pagoda

Holiday Inn Park View, 11 Cavenagh Road (tel: 733 8333). Just off Orchard Road, 320 rooms, business and fitness centres and restaurants serving Western, Chinese and Indian food. Competitive, moderate prices.

Hyatt Regency, 10–12 Scotts Road (tel: 738 1234). Huge hotel complex with over 700 rooms, yet managing to retain a friendly atmosphere. Best rooms are in the Regency Terrace wing, built around the swimming pools with their tropical ambience. Excellent sports facilities, including tennis and squash courts. Brannigan's, the hotel's basement pub, is one of Singapore's best bars, popular with young professionals. For restaurants, choose between Ru Yi for excellent lunchtime *dian xin*, the Lounge for popular high teas and the adventurous Nutmegs, specialising in Californian cuisine. Expensive.

King's Hotel Clarion, 403 Havelock Road (tel: 733 0011). One of a cluster of relatively new hotels on Havelock Road, 300 rooms, popular with Japanese visitors and with above average restaurants serving *dian xin* at lunchtime, plus *sushi* and *teppanyaki*. Moderate prices.

Ladyhill, 1 Ladyhill Road (tel: 737 2111). Tucked away on a quiet road not far from the highly regarded Shangri-La, this moderately priced hotel has a loyal clientele who like its lack of bustle and the friendly staff. Some of the 170 rooms open on to the pool area. Good Swiss restaurant, Le Chalet.

Mandarin Singapore, 333 Orchard Road (tel: 737 4411). Luxury and first-class service at a price; popular with business travellers and well-heeled shoppers. Non-smoking floors, business and fitness centres, and tennis facilities. If you can't afford to stay, go for the excellent local dishes served at the hotel's 24-hour coffee-shop, Chatterbox.

Marina Mandarin, Marina Square, 6 Raffles Boulevard (tel: 338 3388). Sister hotel to the Mandarin Singapore and one of

Tea-time at Goodwood Park Hotel

three hotels sitting above the vast Marina Square shopping complex. Spacious rooms and good sports facilities including swimming pool, gym, tennis and squash courts. The English-style Cricketer Bar is a popular after-work watering hole for expatriates. Good Italian and Chinese restaurants. Expensive.
Le Meridien, 100 Orchard Road (tel: 733 8855). 400-room hotel with a very good French restaurant – Le Restaurant de France – and Gallic cultural pretensions, including occasional art exhibitions and classical concerts. Business and fitness centres, squash and tennis courts. Expensive.
Miramar, 401 Havelock Road (tel: 733 0222). 340 rooms, health club and business centre. Moderate prices.
Novotel Orchid, 214 Dunearn Road (tel: 250 3322). Lively 470-room hotel with one of Singapore's best Szechuan

restaurants, the Dragon City. Suffers from being regarded as 'out of town', though less than 10 minutes by taxi from Orchard Road. Moderate prices but discounts are common.

Omni Marco Polo, 247 Tanglin Road (tel: 474 7141). A 600-room hotel with a lively bistro-style French restaurant, La Brasserie, perennially popular with local gourmets. Best rooms are those set around the poolside terrace. Fitness and business centres, gardens. Expensive.

Orchard Parade, 1 Tanglin Road (tel: 737 1133). Smaller hotel at 300 rooms, with a more intimate atmosphere and perfect for Orchard Road shopping. Popular with European visitors. Moderate prices.

Oriental, Marina Square, 5 Raffles Avenue (tel: 338 0066). Leads off the giant Marina Square shopping complex. Efficient and sophisticated hotel, popular with business travellers. 500 rooms, including no-smoking floors, tennis and squash courts, fitness and business centres, and a good choice of bars and restaurants. Expensive.

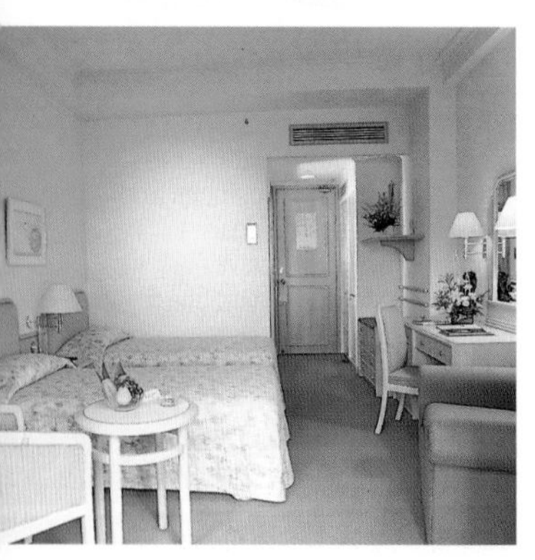

Pan Pacific, Marina Square, 7 Raffles Boulevard (tel: 336 8111). Largest of the three Marina Square hotels, aimed at business travellers, with a 24-hour business centre and up-to-the-minute financial news services. Fine views from the more expensive upper storeys. Good sports facilities, including pool,

King's Hotel's international comfort

Taking a dip at the Hyatt Regency

gym, sauna, tennis and squash courts, and good Cantonese, Continental and Polynesian restaurants. Expensive.

Raffles, 1 Beach Road (tel: 337 1886). The Raffles Hotel was built as the home of a British captain. The Sarkie brothers, immigrants from Armenia, opened its doors as a hotel in 1887. For the next half-century it served as the focus of European social life in the colony. Kipling, Conrad and Somerset Maugham were among the many famous guests. A comprehensive restoration programme has arrested the decline that set in in the 1980s. The fabric has been completely restored and guests now enjoy expensive suites richly furnished and redolent of an age of ocean transport, with state-of-the-art facilities carefully disguised behind the pre-war ambience.

Regent, 1 Cuscaden Road (tel: 733 8888). Luxury hotel popular with business travellers and the well-heeled, just off Orchard Road with business and fitness centres and excellent restaurants, including a branch of Maxim's de Paris. Interesting exhibitions of local artists' work are held in the hotel entrance hall.

River View, 382 Havelock Road (tel: 732 9922). This 480-room hotel has no-smoking floors and expansive views of the Singapore River from many of the rooms. Gardens, fitness centre and restaurants serving local, European, Chinese and Japanese food. Moderate prices.

Royal Holiday Inn Crowne Plaza, 25 Scotts Road (tel: 737 7966). Bustling 500-room hotel, rated one of the best in the worldwide Holiday Inn chain. Facilities include swimming pool, fitness centre, and good restaurants serving Western and Szechuan food. Expensive.

Shangri-La, 22 Orange Grove Road (tel: 737 3644). This luxury hotel is considered the best in Singapore. It does not feel large, despite its 800-plus rooms, because the hotel is spread around a large and well-landscaped tropical garden. Rooms in the Garden Wing have relaxing views of tree-fringed pools and rooms in the Valley Wing are unusually spacious. Sports facilities include two large swimming pools, squash and tennis courts and a pitch and putt golf course. The hotel's excellent French restaurant, Latour, combines top-class cuisine with relaxing informality.

Sheraton Towers, 39 Scotts Road (tel: 737 6888). 400 rooms with no-smoking floors. Excellent and attentive service makes up for rather lack-lustre room décor. Swimming pool, gym, sauna, the Domus Italian restaurant and a very good Cantonese restaurant, Li Bai. Moderate prices.

Sloane Court, 17 Balmoral Road (tel: 235 3311). Tiny hotel with only 32 rooms and one of the best value in Singapore. Clean, comfortable and highly recommended to budget travellers.

Westin Plaza and Westin Stamford, Raffles City, 2 Stamford Road (tel: 338 8585). Two linked hotels with a staggering total of 2,050 rooms, towering above the bustling Raffles City shopping complex. The Westin Stamford, at 73 storeys, is claimed to be the world's tallest hotel and there are magnificent views to be had from many of the rooms. The complex is vast and yet never feels it, so service remains civilised and personal, even when the hotel is full (as it often is with conference delegates from around the world). There is a choice of several restaurants ranging across the world's cuisine. Swimming pools, tennis and squash courts, and 24-hour business centre. Expensive.

Hostel

Singapore International YMCA, 1 Orchard Road, Singapore 0923 (tel: 336 6000). Centrally located. Facilities include swimming pool, squash/ badminton courts. Single or double rooms or communal dormitories. Book well in advance to be sure of getting in.

Dragon dance in the Chingay Parade

CULTURE, ENTERTAINMENT, NIGHTLIFE

Singapore caters for popular rather than sophisticated tastes. You will never be stuck for something to do of an evening, but you will find little by way of cultural events that are demanding or experimental. Nor will you find the kind of raunchy amusement associated with Bangkok or Manila – for that you will have to cross the causeway to the Mechinta nightclub in Johor Baru. The hottest spot in town used to be Bugis Street where visitors, starved of anything more risqué, would pay high prices for drinks to watch the transvestites and drag queens perform. Bugis Street was bulldozed when the MRT was built but the authorities have since rebuilt the street and it has reopened as a new version of Asia's famous entertainment spot. Improvements include a small theatre; it is much cleaner and apparently has an even better atmosphere than the old Bugis Street. World-class entertainers occasionally perform at Singapore's National Stadium or at the biennial Singapore Festival of Arts.

If you want formal entertainment, scan the pages of the *Straits Times* for adverts and reviews. Otherwise you could do what the locals do, especially on a Saturday night: start with drinks in a music bar, go on to dinner and then head for the disco.

Cinema

Singaporeans are great movie-goers and sophisticated multiscreen complexes (such as

Golden Village Yishun 10, Lido 5 Cineplex, Jurong 4 Cineplex and others) offer a wide range of films in air-conditioned comfort. The *Straits Times* lists films in more than 50 cinemas. Modern and classic films of special merit are screened at the Picturehouse in Dhoby Ghaut (tel: 338 3400) and Jade Classics at 100 Beach Road (tel: 293 2581).

Classical Music

The Singapore Symphony Orchestra, founded in 1979, gives regular concerts at the Victoria Concert Hall, (sometimes accompanied by the Singapore Symphony Chorus and sometimes with guest conductors or soloists) and other venues.

Well-known classics are the staple but the orchestra usually includes one adventurous piece in its programme, including works that bridge Eastern and Western musical traditions. For information on forthcoming concerts tel: 338 1230. Tickets can be bought from the Victoria Theatre box office or from the ticket agencies at Tangs department store and Centrepoint, both situated in Orchard Road.

Discos

The disco is Singapore's favourite form of mass entertainment and though the sounds may be international, the etiquette is wholly Singaporean. Members of the 'in crowd' go to see and be seen. If you are a rising young executive, you dress to flaunt your success and wealth (some even take their mobile phones and Filofaxes along). Jeans and T-shirts are out and nobody would dream of dressing outrageously; the aim is to show that you belong, not to stand out. You visit in groups and stay with your group, occasionally hailing friends. Mixing is out and so is overt affection – boys and girls tend to talk rather than kiss and cuddle. Admission prices usually include a free first drink. Prices are high and go up on Fridays and Saturdays, though women may get in for less. High prices are designed to keep out riff-raff, and the 'in crowd' would not have it otherwise; after all, the fact that you can part with a substantial sum for admission and drinks is another sign of your status.

Having said that, if all you want to do is dance and have fun, you will find that nearly every hotel has an unpretentious disco where you can do just that at a fraction of the price.

Caesar's, 02–04 Orchard Towers, 400 Orchard Road (tel: 737 7665). Toga-clad waitresses and live bands interspersed with recorded music.

Chinoiserie, Hyatt Hotel, 10–12 Scotts Road (tel: 733 1188). Formerly a members-only club, now open to all-comers provided they are well heeled and smartly dressed. Comfortable seating for oldies who prefer to watch the action on the small dance floor.

Elvis Place, 298 Beach Road (tel: 299 8403). Retro atmosphere with hits from the 50s and 60s amidst décor devoted to the 'King'.

J.D.'s Pub and Bistrotheque, 180 Orchard Road, Peranakan Place (tel: 732 6966). Combined pub, bistro, disco and karaoke bar. Live bands at 21.00hrs.

Scandals, Westin Stamford Hotel, 2 Stamford Plaza (tel: 338 8585). Sophisticated and elegant, with a mirrored interior, plenty of seating. The club also has a strict dress code.

Top Ten, 04–35 Orchard Towers, 400 Orchard Road (tel: 732 3077). This has been the place to go and be seen ever since it opened in 1985 in a converted cinema decorated with a view of the Manhattan skyline. Guest appearances by top Asian performers at weekends will probably guarantee that it remains the 'in' place.

Warehouse, 332 Havelock Road (tel: 732 9922). Next to the Riverview Hotel, this is the largest and arguably the best disco in town. It is located in a converted *godown* (warehouse) which retains its old-fashioned façade, but features a giant video screen and huge dance floor within.

Xanadu, Shrangri-La Hotel, 22 Orange Grove Road (tel: 737 3644). Up-market, with a slightly older clientele. Art deco-inspired interior with mirrored dance floor, lasers and videos.

Drama, Ballet, Musicals

Local plays, musicals and ballets as well as international productions are staged at a variety of venues such as The Drama Centre, Canning Rise (tel: 336 0005), the Victoria Theatre at Empress Place (tel: 336 7633), The Substation, Armenian Street (tel: 337 7800), The Black Box in Canning Park (tel: 338 6735) and the Harbour Pavilion (tel: 321 2783). The Nanyang Academy of Fine Arts' Chinese Orchestra and the People's Association both have frequent concerts of classical and folk music, often using traditional Chinese instruments (for information tel: 339 5753).

Go down to the Warehouse Disco, the largest in town

Peking opera is very popular in Singapore

Traditional opera thrives in Chinatown, where temporary outdoor theatres are set up near markets and temples. Opera is performed all year round, but the best chance of seeing one is during one of the major festivals such as the Festival of the Hungry Ghosts (see **Special Events**). You may not want to sit through a whole performance, but you should at least sample the colourful, noisy and dramatic action and view the glittering costumes and vivid make-up masks.

Cultural shows Cultural shows provide a painless introduction to the traditional performing arts of Southeast Asia. They are colourful, entertaining and popular with tour groups and children. Ticket prices include a sit-down, buffet or barbecue dinner featuring regional dishes, though you can usually book tickets just for the show.

ASEAN Night Mandarin Hotel, Orchard Road. Poolside barbecue and show featuring dance, music and song from the six ASEAN nations (Singapore, Malyasia, Thailand, Indonesia, Brunei and the Philippines). Every evening except Monday; dinner 19.00hrs, show 19.45hrs. Bookings tel: 737 4411.

Instant Asia Chinese Lion Dance, Malay Harvest Dance and Indian snake charmers. Daily, 11.45hrs at the Cockpit Hotel, Oxley Rise. Bookings tel: 737 9111. Nightly, dinner

18.00hrs, show 20.00hrs at the Singa Inn Seafood Restaurant, 920 East Coast Parkway. Bookings tel: 345 1111.
Lion City Review Cockpit Hotel, Oxley Rise. Local dance, music and song. Daily, dinner 19.00hrs, show 20.00hrs. Bookings tel: 737 9111.
Malam Singapura (Singapore Night) Hyatt Regency, Scotts Road. Poolside show featuring dances from the main ethnic peoples of Singapore: Lion Dance, Fan Dance, Peacock Dance and Malay Wedding. Daily, except Sunday, dinner 19.00hrs, show 20.00hrs. Bookings tel: 738 1234.

Hotel Events

Nearly every hotel has a resident band or pianist but they also sponsor occasional performances by visiting artistes as well; anything from light opera to a Noel Coward play or a chamber quartet. Look for posters around town or check the *Straits Times* for further information.

Karaoke Bars

Though not everyone's idea of entertainment, this Japanese export has caught on in a big way in Singapore. Amateurs from the audience sing along to backing tracks of popular songs assisted by a little electronic mixing to help them sound like stars. Now and then a naturally gifted singer takes to the stage and reduces everyone to tears, compensating for the painful crooning of the majority. If you think you might like this, try the **Joyful Karaoke Lounge**, Concorde Hotel Shopping Centre, 317 Outram Road (tel: 736 0501), where Singapore Broadcasting Corporation artistes perform on Friday evenings.

Pubs and Bars

Singaporean pubs have little in common with their English counterparts. Beer drinkers are in the minority – long cocktails being the order of the day; most provide waiter service and some impose a cover charge. Pubs and bars are open from noon to the small hours of the morning. Happy hour is generally from 17.30 to 19.30hrs when you can buy two drinks for the price of one. Prices are high – liquor (beer, wines and spirits) being one of the few commodities that are subject to import duty. Pubs and bars are not ideal for quiet conversation. Nearly all provide music, either from a live band or on video. Pick your pub according to your taste in music.
Anywhere, 04–08 Tanglin Shopping Centre, 19 Tanglin Road (tel: 734 8233). Popular and lively bar where extrovert and versatile bands perform anything from Bob Dylan to heavy metal and rock and roll on Saturday nights (closed Sunday); relatively inexpensive.
Brannigan's, Hyatt Regency Hotel, 10–12 Scotts Road (tel: 733 1188). Very popular after-work meeting place located in the basement for singles of all nationalities. Good live music with audience participation and bar food. Usually packed out by 20.00hrs.
Casablanca Wine Bar, 7 Emerald Hill Road (tel: 733 6716). Small and friendly wine

bar at the back of this excellent French restaurant, converted from an old Straits-Chinese terraced house. Favourite expatriate haunt.

Cheers, Novotel Orchid Inn, Dunearn Road (tel: 250 3322). Entertaining bar with a slightly camp atmosphere. Music from the two live bands and from the singing waiters.

Compass Rose, Westin Stamford Hotel, 2 Stamford Road (tel: 338 8585). Located on the 72nd floor of the hotel, this circular bar with glass walls is well worth visiting just for the panoramic views which, on a clear day, stretch as far as Malaysia and Indonesia. However, it can get very crowded at weekends and you will not be let in if you are wearing a T-shirt or shorts.

Harry's Quayside Café, 28 Boat Quay (tel: 538 3029). Popular American jazz pub and café overlooking the Singapore River. Western cuisine with live jazz, jam sessions on Sunday from 19.00hrs.

Raffles Hotel, 1 Beach Road (tel: 337 1886). This is the new place to be seen in town. There are two bars, the Long Bar and the Bar and Billiard Room (where the billiard tables are always in use); both bars have colonial décor.

Saxophone Bar and Restaurant, 23 Cuppage Terrace (tel: 235 8385). Choose between tables on the pavement, seats in the tiny high-ceilinged bar or a meal in the upstairs bistro to the accompaniment of live jazz on Wednesday through to Saturday nights. The special atmosphere and the excellence of the local musicians have made this place famous worldwide, and even big-name stars drop by to jam in the cramped surroundings when they are in town.

Somerset's Bar, Westin Stamford Hotel, 2 Stamford Road (tel: 338 8585). Old colonial décor and excellent live jazz, especially popular on Sundays.

Wine Lovers, 18 Lorong Mambong, Holland Village (tel: 462 4510). Spanish bar and brasserie, with lunch served from noon and tapas available throughout the day. Spanish music.

Theatre Restaurants

Two decades ago these provided slightly risqué floor shows aimed at Chinese businessmen entertaining their clients. Today they still attract a predominantly Chinese clientele but the cabaret is more likely to feature top singers and entertainers from Hong Kong or Taiwan. The décor is plush, the food usually excellent and the prices on the high side, but if you are too old for the disco and want to see where local Chinese go for a special night out, you could gather together a party of friends.

Lido Palace Nite-CLub, Concorde Hotel,317 Outram Road, tel: 732 8855. Features local TV stars, live bands, a disco and lavish Cantonese banquets.

Neptune Theatre Restaurant, 50 Collyer Quay (tel: 224 3922 for information and reservations). The largest theatre restaurant in Singapore with dazzling cabaret routines and top-class Cantonese cuisine.

WEATHER AND WHEN TO GO

Singapore is located 85 miles (136km) north of the equator and the climate has little seasonal variation. Typically, the temperature rises to 30.6°C/87°F at noon – but this is an average, and some days it can be several degrees higher. It is slightly cooler from November to January, when the temperature can fall to 24°C/75°F, comfortable for a northern European, but regarded as chilly by Singaporeans (but also welcomed as an opportunity for the ladies to get out their expensive and little-used fur coats). This is also the wettest period, though it does not rain for a very prolonged period; spectacular thunderstorms can greet the dawn or tear the skies open in mid-afternoon, causing anyone who is out in the open to flee for shelter, but the torrent is usually over in an hour. July is the driest month, but the humidity tends to remain high, at around 85 per cent, throughout the year. To cope with the climate, all hotels (except the cheapest), restaurants, shopping arcades and taxis have air-conditioning. Out of doors you need very light easily washed clothing, but the air-conditioning indoors can make the air so cold that you will benefit from a jacket or wrap. The lack of climatic variation, and the fact that the tropical vegetation is always verdant and colourful (there is no autumn), means that Singapore is an all-year-round destination. It is more difficult, however, to find cheap flights and hotel rooms in the months of December, January and February. Partly this is because many Asians visit Singapore during the Christmas and Chinese New Year holidays, and partly because the air routes to Europe are heavily used by Singaporean expatriates coming home, or by Europeans flying via Singapore to visit Australia and New Zealand.

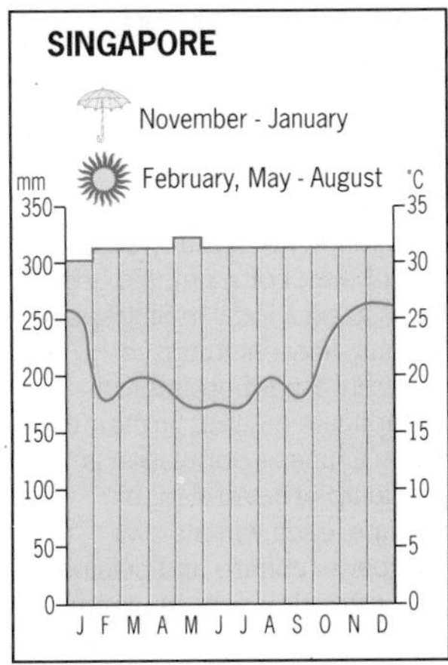

HOW TO BE A LOCAL

Singapore's population is made up of 77 per cent Chinese, 14 per cent Malay and 7 per cent Indian, with the balance of 2 per cent made up of Europeans and members of other ethnic groups. Thus to be a local in Singapore means different things to different Singaporeans. To complicate matters further, the large Chinese population is made up of several ethnic groups, each with its own language, culture and cuisine; some are Hokkienese, some Teochew, others Cantonese, and then there is the small élite group of Straits-Chinese, the descendants of early Chinese settlers who intermarried with local Malays. Such is the diversity that the Government has mounted a propaganda campaign to persuade all Chinese Singaporeans to learn and speak Mandarin, one of the four official languages of Singapore (along with Malay, English and Tamil). You are quite likely to see posters in shops and restaurants exhorting people to 'Speak Mandarin – do not use dialects'. The command is more often broken than obeyed. The older generation of Singaporean Chinese – the taxi driver or the hawker stall proprietor – has little formal education and is not likely to have studied Mandarin. They will speak a mother tongue and enough English to deal with visitors on a commercial basis. The post-war generation, the beneficiaries of an excellent education programme, will speak English by preference and as a matter of pride and status, for a good command of English is essential for a successful career with one of Singapore's multi-national enterprises and marks you out as upwardly mobile. Mandarin conveys no such advantages but is gaining importance with increasing business ties with Taiwan and China. Amongst themselves, young Chinese may also speak Singaporean English, or 'Singlish'. Educated Chinese look down on this patois which mixes English, Chinese and Malay words but is spoken with Chinese intonation and sentence structure, as in 'Ai kee Madonna mai?', meaning 'Are you coming to McDonalds?', or 'Early-early

Hawker food centres are good value

don't say?', which means 'Why didn't you say so before?'. Singlish is regarded as shopgirl talk, but even the most sophisticated Chinese will occasionally end a sentence with the exclamation 'la!', spoken with a rising interrogative tone and inviting the listener to agree with the statement.

Older Chinese are more likely to keep up traditional religious practices. They may have a shrine in their kitchen to the household gods, who report back to the spirit world on the behaviour of the family and hand out appropriate rewards or punishments. To them the spirit world is none the less real for being invisible, and you may find that a taxi driver is reluctant to go to certain places on the island after dark (especially those associated with wartime atrocities) because of bad spirits. Younger Chinese are less likely to adhere to the old ways, though they respect them, and would be offended if they were described as primitive or superstitious. They will also be very family-orientated and respectful of their elders. Big family reunions are commonplace and you will frequently see several generations of one family sit down together for a restaurant banquet. Younger Chinese also retain a vestigial sense that nothing happens except by permission of the gods – though they may not express it in such terms. Instead, they will avoid arrogance or hubris, and they also tend to be much more deferential to authority than Westerners. There are, however, several corollaries to this. One is that nobody will accept personal responsibility for a mistake – they will always blame it on someone or something else. Westerners can easily give offence by singling out some individual for blame, causing loss of 'face'. Another is that respect for authority leads to excessive status-consciousness and an exaggerated regard for the outward trappings of success. The large number of expensive boutiques in Singapore selling designer-label fashions and accessories would not be able to survive on the tourist trade alone; Chinese Singaporeans enhance their status literally by wearing their success on their sleeves, and they do not understand why many Western visitors dress so casually by comparison (it was not so long ago that Singaporean immigration officials forced long-haired visitors to have a short back-and-sides before letting them into the country).

The Malay community is marked by similar generational differences to the Chinese. Older Malays will be devoutly religious and their lives will revolve around the mosque or neighbourhood self-help groups. The latter are a reflection of the old *Kampong* lifestyle, a reminder that Singaporean Malays used to live in small, tight-knit communities. Now that they have been rehoused in Government apartment blocks, the old self-help ethic expresses itself through these committees, which do much good in helping Malay children with their education (providing special classes in English or computers, for example) and in keeping Malay traditions alive. Young Malays are less likely to read the Koran or go to Friday prayers, but because they come from such close communities, even the most Westernised Malay finds it difficult to shake off old customs. They will still observe Islamic food laws, for example, and not eat pork or drink alcohol. Many still observe the daylight fast of Ramadan, just as many non church-going Christians still give up something for Lent. Younger Malays are more integrated into Singaporean society but they may still face a degree of latent prejudice from the Chinese, who traditionally regarded them as less hard working. Indeed, it has been true in the past that Malay children have not been so successful at school as their Chinese contemporaries, but the Council for the Education of Malay Children has done much to resolve this problem and, increasingly, you will meet well-educated Malays who work in positions of influence in government and commerce.

Most of the Indians in Singapore today are Hindu Tamils and, whilst visitors tend to think that the community is concentrated in the colourful Little India quarter, you will, in fact, find Indians everywhere in Singapore; working as money changers and newspaper vendors, selling carpets, textiles, leather goods and watches in every shopping centre. In other words, with their commercial skills and fluency in English, many of Singapore's Indians have chosen to be self-employed entrepreneurs, although the younger generation increasingly favours jobs in the civil service or the professions.

All three communities contribute to the rich cultural life of the island; temples and festivals are among the island's chief attractions. Visitors are welcomed and there are very few rules; shoes must be removed on entering mosques or Hindu temples, women must dress modestly to enter a mosque and may not enter certain clearly signposted areas, and photography is not normally permitted during worship,

Consult the augurs, at a price

Even the shops display Singaporean love of elegance

although exceptions are made for the big festivals; at other times it is polite to ask before using your camera. Otherwise, provided that you behave with normal politeness and courtesy, you are rarely likely to give offence in Singapore. However, you will frequently be asked if you are enjoying yourself and, although Singaporeans are increasingly critical of themselves, their society and their government (and you may well enjoy a good political debate with your taxi-driver), to say 'no' would be to risk causing both puzzlement and offence to a people who pride themselves on their hospitality, even when it does have a commercial motive, and who themselves, whether they be Chinese, Indian or Malay, are also very proud to be Singaporean.

The flume ride at Haw Par Villa/ Dragon World is just one of many attractions which will appeal to children

CHILDREN

Getting to Singapore with children may not be one of the most enjoyable of experiences if taking a long-haul flight. Once there, however, and with the tedium of the journey forgotten, it is very easy for parents and children to have fun in Singapore. It is a safe city, with little violent crime, and you need have no qualms about letting teenagers explore on their own; they will no doubt master the transport system faster than you, make friends quickly and return full of stories of their adventures.

If they are of disco-going age (and these days that can mean very young), tea-dances are a good way of making friends and having fun; several discos host these events, where the music, video and sound shows are the same as at night but the drinks are non-alcoholic. One of the most popular venues is **Five Discotheque** (150 Orchard Road, tel: 235 0155 – tea dances 14.00–18.00hrs on Saturday and Sunday) which has two dance floors, a pub and karaoke.

Singaporeans often eat out together as one big happy family, including everyone from grandparents down to three- or four-year olds, so eating out with children is never a problem, except in some of the more exclusive restaurants.

Children may not like the more spicy foods, but *satay* is popular and there is usually a chicken dish on the menu that they will like. There are also scores of fast food outlets in Singapore, and you are never far away from a Pizza Hut or McDonald's restaurant.

The sights of Singapore seem almost purpose-designed with children in mind (in a sense they are, since a third of Singapore's population is less than 20 years of age). Top attractions for the young are the Zoological Gardens, Sentosa Island, the Guinness World of Records and the Singapore Science Centre – full of push-button working models, but also full of other children who all want a go. A must for all children is the Haw Par Villa/Dragon World, especially a ride on the Wrath of the Water Gods Flume, though it does usually mean a lengthy wait in the queue. (See entries in **What to See** section.)

Singapore has some spectacular swimming pools, with wave pools and water slides, where children can cool off and burn up their energies without offending anyone, whereas they may not be welcome to do so at a hotel pool. One is the **Big Splash**, East Coast Parkway (tel: 345 1211), *open*: Monday to Friday 12.00–17.45hrs and weekends 09.00–17.45hrs (10.00–17.45hrs during school holidays).

Most hotels will provide a baby-sitting service – just ask at the concierge desk – given a day's notice. You will find that baby-sitting staff are very trustworthy, if a little indulgent towards their charges.

TIGHT BUDGET

The biggest problem facing those travelling in Singapore on a budget is finding low-cost accommodation.

Your best bet is the YMCA Singapore International, 1 Orchard Road, Singapore 0923 (tel: 336 6000). The location of the YMCA is very central and the facilities, including a swimming pool and squash/badminton courts, are almost as good as those of a much more expensive hotel.

Needless to say, it is very popular and bookings should be made well in advance.

Accommodation is in single rooms or double rooms or, cheapest of all, in communal dormitories. If you cannot get into the YMCA, try the Sloane Court Hotel (see **Accommodation** section) or check at the airport hotel-booking desk on arrival to see what last-minute discounts are on offer.

Otherwise, Singapore is a very cheap destination. You can eat your fill of exotic foods at hawker food stalls for a minimal sum. Travel by bus or MRT rarely costs more than a dollar or so for individual journeys and an inexpensive Singapore Explorer bus pass will give you unlimited travel for one or three days for a few dollars.

Your best chance of meeting local people is in bars or discos, but these do not come cheap. Take advantage of bar happy hours, when the drinks are cheaper, and go to the disco on Mondays to Thursdays, when the entrance prices are lower.

SPECIAL EVENTS

The ethnic and religious diversity of Singapore guarantees that the calendar is crowded with festivals. The Malay, Chinese and Indian communities not only celebrate the days that are of special significance to them, they also come together for big festivals – such as the Chingay Parade or National Day – that unite the whole island in festivity. It is difficult to give precise dates for many events because they are based on lunar calendars; to add to the confusion, these vary from each other as well as from the Western calendar. The best way to find out what is going on is to get the free leaflet available from the Singapore Tourist Promotion Board, giving dates and useful guidance on the significance of the island's many festivals.

New Year's Eve: the New Year of the Western calendar is essentially a time for private parties. Ships moored in the harbour blow their foghorns at midnight to welcome in the new year.

Ponggal (mid January): this Tamil harvest festival marks the beginning of spring and the end of the rainy season in southern India, traditionally a time for spring-cleaning and donning new clothes. *Ponggal* is a dish of newly harvested rice cooked with nuts, peas, raisins and milk. The pot is allowed to boil over, symbolically representing a plentiful harvest, before being presented to the sun god. This is essentially a family festival but you can watch rice being blessed, accompanied by the music of drums, bells and conch shells, at the Perumal Temple in Serangoon Road.

Thaipusam (January/February): this is Singapore's most spectacular Tamil festival, but not one that the squeamish will relish.

Devotees work themselves into a trance and pierce their bodies with all manner of hooks and skewers in the hope that the Hindu deity, Lord Muruga (also known as Lord Subramanya), will reward their courage by granting their desires. The festival begins at the Perumal Temple in Serangoon Road where the skin-piercing takes place.

Participants then process to the Chettiar Temple in Tank Road, some of them walking on spiked sandals and some carrying a heavy metal frame, called a *kadavi*, decorated with flowers and peacock feathers. The route of the procession is published in the *Straits Times* and large crowds gather to accompany the devotees on their painful pilgrimage, encouraging them with chanting and traditional songs.

Chinese New Year (late January/early February) since some 76 per cent of Singapore's population is Chinese, the beginning of the lunar new year is the island's most important holiday, and it is the only time of year when you are likely to find shops closed and taxis elusive. To compensate for that, you will find that Chinatown comes alive – not just for the New Year but for several days beforehand. The streets and shops are decorated with lights and red banners and street hawkers sell seasonal delicacies, such as barbecued pork and duck, from pavement stalls. Flower shops do a brisk trade selling potted mandarin and plum trees, both of which are associated with good fortune; mandarin fruits because they are the colour of gold, and plum blossoms because their fresh blooms promise renewal and new life. The Chinese New Year is greeted by noisy celebrations; malign spirits that are said to roam at the time of the new moon are frightened by light, noise and the colour red, hence the blaze of colour and light in Chinatown. Traditionally the spirits are kept at bay by setting off explosive firecrackers, but Singapore prohibits such a dangerous practice. You will, however, find plenty of good-humoured drum- and gong-banging as an accompaniment to the lion and dragon dances that take place in the streets of Chinatown before and during the festival.

For the Chinese themselves, New Year is a time for family reunions and present-giving; all unmarried children receive *hong bao*, gifts of money distributed in red and gold packets by their married brothers. Staff receive a pay bonus from their employers and many businesses still observe the tradition of clearing all their bills and debts by the eve of New Year. It is also a time for renewal; literally for spring-cleaning and redecorating the home, for buying new furniture and new clothes – so the shops are more crowded than usual in the run up to the holiday.

Chingay (February): this parade marks the end of the New Year festivities and is usually held on the first (though sometimes the second) Sunday after Chinese New Year's Day. The parade begins at 09.00hrs, starting at the Scotts Road junction and passing down Orchard Road to end at Clemenceau Avenue. Everyone takes part – Malay, Indian and European as well as Chinese – and the parade is a spectacular *mélange* of carnival floats, stilt walkers and dance troupes who perform everything from dragon dances to English morris.

Monkey God Feast (March and September): in Chinese

Chinese Garden's creative crockery

mythology the monkey is a symbol of intelligence and wit – a survivor who will always get his way in the end by skill, guile, bravery and endurance. The Monkey King is revered as a human role model and is credited with healing powers. Those who take part in the Monkey God Feast seek to become mediums through which the spirit of the god will perform good acts. The feast is celebrated twice a year at the Monkey God Temple in Seng Poh Road. Participants carry a sedan chair which they throw about as if it were occupied by the twitching, lively, ever-active Monkey King. They then skewer their cheeks and tongues and cut their skin so as to write charms with their blood – charms which are supposed to bring good fortune to the recipients. Like Thaipusam, this is not a festival for the faint-hearted.

Qing Ming (March/April): this festival brings Chinese families together to honour their ancestors, specifically by visiting their graves and making offerings of food and gifts of money, motor cars, video cameras and TV sets – not the real thing, of course, but paper models that are burned on the graves to allow them to pass into the spirit world.

Ramadan (March/April): the Muslim month of daytime abstinence from food is, for visitors, chiefly an occasion for sampling the Malay delicacies with which Muslims break their fast after dark. Food stalls are set up around mosques and one of the best places to go, for the atmosphere and for a range of unusual sweetmeats, is Bussorah Street, near the Sultan Mosque.

Hari Raya Puasa (April): this festival marks the end of Ramadan and is the most important holiday in the Muslim calendar. As with Chinese New Year it is an occasion for family reunions. Geylang Serai, the area south of Geylang Road on Singapore's East Coast (Paya Lebar MRT station) is the district that most retains its Malay character. At Hari Raya Puasa, and for several days after, the streets are ablaze with festive lights and street markets are set up selling everything from traditional Malay delicacies to kites, rugs, jewellery and brightly coloured fabrics.

Vesak Day (May): this most important day in the Buddhist calendar marks the anniversary of the birth, enlightenment and death of the Buddha. At the Temple of a Thousand Lights, in Race Course Road, you can watch the initiation ceremonies of new Buddhist devotees and share in the vegetarian feast that is distributed to all-comers. Another moving ceremony is the candle-lit procession that takes place in the temple courtyard on the evening of Vesak Day.

Dragon Boat Festival (June): originally this festival commemorated the death of the poet Qu Yuan who drowned himself in protest against the corruption that was rife in the China of his time. The fishermen who witnessed the event raced out in their boats to try and prevent his suicide and then, by beating drums, thrashing the surface of the water and

Singapore's multi-ethnic community celebrates numerous festivals

throwing handfuls of rice, tried to prevent his body being consumed by fish until it could be rescued. Chinese communities have honoured the poet's death ever since by holding boat races and the event now attracts teams from all over the world who specialise in the sport. The 40-foot- (12m) long boats retain their original form, with a dragon's head at the prow, and the oarsmen are encouraged in their strenuous efforts by a drummer who sits at the prow and by the cheers of supporters who follow the races in a flotilla of boats.

Hari Raya Haji (June): this Muslim religious festival is a day of prayer followed by the ritual slaughter of sheep and cattle, commemorating the prophet Ibrahim's obedience to Allah, who asked the prophet to sacrifice his son and, at the last moment, substituted a sheep. The Sultan Mosque, in North Bridge Road, is the main centre of events.

Festival of the Hungry Ghosts (August): this is the time of year at which restless spirits roam the earth, especially those who received no burial, who died violently, whose families have neglected to perform their obligations to the dead or whose earthly misdeeds have resulted in their condemnation to the Chinese equivalent of Purgatory. To appease these spirits, who can wreak mischief and bring misfortune to the mortal world, pious Chinese mount small altars in front of their homes on which they place offerings of apples and oranges, joss sticks and paper money – all intended to placate or distract the wandering spirits.

The festival is also accompanied by performances of Chinese opera, or *wayang*; stages are set up near food centres, markets and temples, especially in

Chinatown, and you will not have to look far to witness this colourful and dramatic spectacle.

National Day (9 August): the huge and spectacular National Day parade takes place, in alternate years, in the National Stadium or on the Padang and it celebrates the anniversary of Singapore's independence, 9 August 1965. The parade is accompanied by military manoeuvres and a fly-past of the Singapore air force, but the highlight is a precision display of choreographed movements in which hundreds of school, community and cultural groups take part, dressed in colourful costumes and waving flags to form patterns representing national symbols. The whole event ends with a huge fireworks display.

Chinese lanterns add a splash of colour to the Mooncake Festival

Mid-autumn (Mooncake) Festival (September/October): there are several different versions of the origins of this festival. One has it that two lovers, who inhabit the sun and moon respectively, separated throughout the rest of the year, are allowed to meet for this one month. Another has it that the festival celebrates the overthrow of Mongol rule in China in the 14th century; messages calling for an uprising were secreted in cakes and distributed throughout the country. Whichever is true, the 15th day of the eighth lunar month is an occasion for families to go out at night with paper lanterns, gaze at the moon and eat mooncakes – pastries filled with an egg yolk or with sweetened red bean or lotus seed paste. You will find lanterns and mooncakes on sale everywhere in Chinatown and the Chinese Garden, in Jurong, is the setting for a colourful lantern festival, where schoolchildren sing traditional songs and perform lion and dragon dances.

Navarathri (Nine Nights) Festival (September/October): this Hindu festival celebrates the three incarnations of the supreme female deity, Devi. In the form of Dhurga, she represents the mother of creation, as Lakshmi she represents wealth and as Saraswathi she is revered as the goddess of learning. The festival centres on the Chettiar Temple in Tank Road where, on each night of the festival between 19.00 and 22.00hrs, devotees praise the deity through traditional music and dance. On the tenth day a silver horse is carried in procession through the streets around the temple.

Thimithi (September/October): in another test of faith and endurance, devotees of the Hindu goddess Draupadi race barefoot across a 12-foot- (4m) long bed of red-hot coals in the courtyard of the Sri Mariamman Temple in South Bridge Road.

Festival of the Nine Emperor Gods (October/November): this Chinese festival honours the nine sons of the Queen of Heaven, sometimes called Kwan Yin, the goddess of mercy. Each son is attributed with a particular power, one bestows wealth, another longevity and another good health. The nine days of the festival are marked with temple ceremonies and performances of Chinese opera. At the culmination of the festival, images of the gods are carried in procession in sedan chairs and devotees whip themselves into a trance in which they commit acts of bravery and self-mutilation. One of the best places to witness the festival is the Kiu Ong Yiah Temple in Upper Serangoon Road.

Kusu Pilgrimage (October/November): during this festival extra ferries are laid on for the journey to the island of Kusu, departing from the World Trade Centre, to accommodate the thousands of Chinese and Malay pilgrims who visit the island's two shrines. Here they offer rice, fruit or bunches of marigolds or chrysanthemums in the hope of achieving prosperity in the year ahead. The trees that line the steps from the Chinese temple on the beach to the Malay shrine on the island's summit are hung with the offerings of the unmarried or childless who hope to marry and/or conceive in the year ahead.

Deepavali (October/November): during this Hindu festival of light the streets of Little India are festooned with street lights, and oil lamps are lit in temples and homes to symbolise the triumph of good over evil, light over dark. Indian families surround the doors of their homes with lights in order to show Lakshmi, the goddess of prosperity, the way to their house. Sweets and delicacies are prepared for the festival and the temples of Little India are filled with sweetly scented flower garlands and fruits, left as offerings to the temple deities.

Christmas (25 December): as elsewhere in the world, Christmas in Singapore has become an excuse for a spending spree; shops and hotels strive to outdo each other in mounting big displays and special events, especially carol concerts. Orchard Road is decorated with festoons of lights and, on Christmas Eve, is closed to traffic so that families can stroll amongst the carolling choirs and take photographs. On a more serious note, local charities put a lot of effort into fundraising at this time of year and raise large sums for worthwhile causes.

SPORT

Many hotels have swimming pools and fitness centres, and several have squash and tennis courts, and these are often as much as any moderately active traveller desires to keep fit. If, however, you are an enthusiast who wants to meet fellow enthusiasts for a particular sport, or if you wish to pit your skills against those of the local people, contact the Singapore Sports Council for information, tel: 345 7111.

Spectator Sports

The venerable **Singapore Cricket Club** holds matches on the Padang between March and October every Saturday from 13.30hrs and every Sunday from 10.30hrs (tel: 338 9367 for information on fixtures). The Padang is also the venue for **rugby matches** from September to March. The pace of the game is somewhat slower under the equatorial sun than it is under European skies, but the atmosphere on the touchline is no different. Matches take place on Saturdays at 16.00 and 17.15hrs.

Horse racing takes place all year round at the beautifully landscaped Singapore Turf Club, Bukit Timah Road (tel: 469 3611), and the races are keenly supported by local people who gamble their hard-earned money in the hope that the gods will be kind and give them instant riches. Several tour operators offer afternoons at the races, including a buffet lunch and use of the members' enclosure, with its grandstand views of the action.

Polo is played regularly from February to October at the Singapore Polo Club, 80 Mount Pleasant Road (tel: 256 4530).

Football matches are staged at the huge National Stadium and fixtures are carried in the *Straits Times*; alternatively you can call the Singapore Sports Council for information (tel: 345 7111).

Participant Sports

Singapore has several fine **golf** courses, but visitors are usually limited to playing on weekdays.

In any event, it is best to telephone and make an advance booking. Some of the best are:
Changi Golf Club, Netheravon Road, tel: 545 5133.
Jurong Country Club 9 Science Centre Road, tel: 560 5655.
Singapore Island Country Club, Upper Thomson Road, tel: 459 2222.
Raffles Country Club, Jalan Ahmad Ibrahim, tel: 861 7655.

Watersports At the **East Coast Sailing Centre**, 1210 East Coast Parkway (tel: 449 5118), you can hire windsurfing equipment and Laser class dinghies. Training courses are also available, but these are usually of two or more days' duration. Members of overseas yacht clubs should contact the **Singapore Yacht Club**, 249 Jalan Buroh (tel: 265 0931) or the **Changi Sailing Club**, 32 Netheravon Road (tel: 545 2876).

In the middle of a chukkar at the Singapore Polo Club

DIRECTORY

Contents

Arriving
Babysitting
Camping
Complaints
Crime
Customs
Disabled People
Driving
Electricity
Embassies
Emergency Telephone Numbers
Entertainment
Guidebooks
Health
Holidays
Lost Property
Media
Money
Opening Times
Personal Safety
Pharmacies
Places of Worship
Police
Post Office
Public Transport
Rules and Regulations
Telephones
Time
Tipping
Toilets
Tourist Offices
Tour Operators
Travel Agencies

Arriving

Passports

Visitors from the EU, US, Australia and New Zealand and most European and Commonwealth countries do not need a visa, just a passport valid for at least six months beyond date of entry. Citizens of India do need a visa, as do Hong Kong visitors travelling on a Certificate of Identity social visit pass. Your passport will be stamped on arrival with a tourist visa allowing you to stay for 30 days. You must apply for an extension if you plan to stay any longer, at the Immigration Office in Singapore, South Bridge Centre (tel: 532 2877).

Health Regulations

No vaccinations are necessary unless you have visited a yellow fever-infected area within the previous six days, or a cholera-infected area within the previous 14 days.

Lion Dances are one manifestation of Singapore's polyglot cultural heritage

By Air

Flying to Singapore is easy enough. There are direct flights from virtually every international airport in the world. The route is heavily used and you have to book well in advance to take advantage of the low-cost flights that are advertised in the newspapers. You should also shop around; cheap flights can be secured if you are prepared to travel with a less well-known airline or put up with an indirect route involving several stops and a longer journey time. If money is less of a consideration, you could do worse than to fly non-stop with the national carrier, Singapore Airlines, widely regarded as one of the world's best.

Equally, Singapore's Changi Airport is one of the most advanced in the world. Business travellers regularly nominate it as their favourite airport in opinion polls.

Changi (or 'Airtropolis', as the marketing people now want us to call it) is a hub airport, so many of its facilities are geared towards transit passengers with an hour or so to kill between flights. Hence there are day rooms and showers, a gym and sauna, a business centre, extensive shopping facilities and a good range of restaurants in both terminals, not to mention a nursery and children's play area.

Airport Tax These services are not entirely free. A departure tax of S$5 is chargeable. Airport tax coupons can be purchased in advance at most hotels, travel agencies and airline offices.

Clearing the Airport The airport runs smoothly despite handling nearly 400 flights a day. Baggage trollies are plentiful and there is no charge for their use. Baggage handling delays are rare, queues at immigration move swiftly and you are not likely to be stopped at customs. Allow about 25 minutes to clear the airport. While you are waiting, look out for free tourist literature, including the *Singapore Official Guide* available from display stands in the arrivals area. You can change money at the airport – in fact, with the authorities controlling prices strictly, it is a good place to buy your dollars. There is also a hotel booking service for those who arrive without a reservation.

City Link Some hotels provide a pick-up service from the airport for those who have made advance arrangements. It is cheaper to go by taxi. There are ranks outside both terminals and the fare to the centre will cost around S$15–25 for a journey of about 20 minutes.

A comfortable and efficient Airbus service operates from the terminal basements to downtown hotels; it runs from 06.20–00.30hrs, approximately every 20 minutes.

By Rail

Trains from Bangkok, Butterworth and Kuala Lumpur arrive at Keppel Road Railway Station, adjacent to Chinatown and the Central Business District. Again, taxis are plentiful and hotels are less than 10 minutes away.

By Road

Avoid arriving by road at weekends when the causeway linking Singapore to peninsular Malaysia is very congested. Express coach services operate from several towns in Malaysia, including Kuala Lumpur, Malacca and Penang (journey time at least seven hours).

By Sea

Cruise liners berth at the new Singapore Cruise Centre next to the World Trade Centre. It is 10 minutes by taxi to/from Orchard Road.

Babysitting

This service is available in most hotels.

Camping

The best campsite is the new, 5-star NTUC Sentosa Beach Resort on Sentosa Island, with good views over the sea. As well as standard chalets it features 15 rustic 'camp shelters', each capable of accommodating up to four people. There is a swimming pool, barbecue pits, and café. NTUC Sentosa Beach Resort, 30 Imbiah Walk, Sentosa (tel: 275 1034).

Chemist see **Pharmacies**

Complaints
If you cannot resolve the matter satisfactorily with the supplier of the goods or services, it is worth lodging your complaint with the Singapore Tourist Promotion Board (tel: 736 6622) or the Consumers' Association of Singapore (tel: 270 4611). Genuine grievances are dealt with swiftly and they will do their best to resolve the matter and to ensure that other visitors do not suffer the same problems.
If necessary you can also seek redress through the Small Claims Tribunal. The tribunal will consider claims up to S$5,000 in value and will usually give a ruling within 24 hours where visitors are involved. Claims can be lodged up to 12 months after the date of purchase, though your presence is required in court. Cases will be heard within two to three days. No legal representation is necessary. A small fee is payable. Forms can be obtained from the Small Claims Tribunal, Apollo Centre, 2 Havelock Road, Singapore (tel: 435 5937).

Crime
Singapore has one of the lowest crime rates in the world and it is safe to go almost anywhere, even at night – police patrols are at their busiest from dusk to dawn. Even so, you should not be foolhardy. Take care of your valuables and do not put temptation in the way of pickpockets.

The futuristic Changi airport is a typically Singaporean model of efficiency

Trishaws are a thing of the past – although still available for tourist jaunts

Customs

Personal possessions are not liable to duty and tax provided that you intend to take them out again. There is no restriction on the amount of money that you can bring into Singapore. Duty-free allowances, granted to visitors over 18 years of age arriving from countries other than Malaysia, are:

Spirits	1 litre
Wine	1 litre
Beer	1 litre

The import of clove cigarettes (*kreteks*), popular in Malaysia and Indonesia, is now banned by the Singapore authorities on health grounds. Other controlled or prohibited items include: all narcotics, arms and explosives, replica firearms, endangered species and their by-products (including ivory), chewing gum and obscene publications (including magazines like *Penthouse*). If you are stopped in customs, special attention will be paid to any tape or video cassettes you may be carrying. Any material that infringes copyright (for example, pirated tapes) or obscenity laws is liable to confiscation.

Certain medicines that are only available on prescription under Singapore law (including sleeping pills, tranquillisers and stimulants) are also likely to arouse suspicion. Singapore customs advise travellers to carry a letter from their doctor confirming that the drugs are medically necessary.

Disabled People

As part of its drive to make Singapore attractive to all visitors, the authorities are very conscious of the needs of disabled travellers. Ramps, elevators and specially designed toilets and telephones are available in many public buildings such as the airport, and in many hotels. You will also find that hotel, restaurant and shop staff are always willing to provide assistance. Getting about by public transport is, however, not so easy and you will definitely need help from your travelling companions to negotiate buses and the MRT. For a detailed guide to easily accessible attractions, ask for the booklet *Access Singapore*, (free of charge) available from the Singapore Council for Social Services, 11 Penang Lane (tel: 336 1544).

Driving

Public transport in Singapore is so good and taxis so cheap that driving is not necessary. If you are in two minds, remember how small Singapore is; you can get from end to end in under an hour and for a taxi fare of around S$60.

Remember, too, that parking downtown is very difficult and that you need to buy a special pass to enter the Central Business District (CBD) between 07.30 and 18.30hrs on weekdays, and between 07.30 and 14.00hrs on Saturdays. This restriction is rigidly enforced; every car entering the CBD is checked and traffic police are generally tough on those who transgress the law.

If you are still determined to drive yourself, you need a valid driver's licence and an international licence.

All the major car rental firms are represented in Singapore as well as many local firms. They are listed in the Singapore *Yellow Pages* under 'Motorcar Renting and Leasing', and it pays to shop around.

If, on the other hand, you want to make an advance reservation and collect your car at the airport, contact Avis on tel: 737 1668 or Hertz tel: 734 4646.

Rules of the Road Traffic drives on the left and the speed limits are 30 mph (50kph) on most roads, rising to 50 mph (80kph) on expressways. The police use video cameras, mounted on traffic lights or along the verge, to record traffic behaviour, so do not think you can break the law just because you cannot see a policeman. You are quite likely to receive a summons or a fine demand through the post if you commit an offence.

The result of such surveillance is that most drivers are courteous and careful, though you do have to remain alert; lane-hoppers, especially laden goods vehicles, are a constant hazard.

Parking Singapore's street parking system can be extremely baffling, even to locals. You have to buy a book of coupons and tear out numbers showing the precise date and time that you parked. Street signs indicate how long you can park for – up to an hour in some places, less in the centre. Traffic police make regular checks and will fine transgressors. Parking is not much easier outside the central area, though some out-of-town housing estates have free parking on Sundays. Licences to enter the Central Business District can be bought from signposted kiosks located around the periphery of the CBD.

Car Breakdown Car rental firms usually operate their own breakdown arrangements. Alternatively, you can telephone the Automobile Association of Singapore's 24-hour road service, tel: 748 9911.

Chauffeur-driven Cars If you need the freedom of private transport and do not want the hassle of driving yourself, you will find that it is easy and inexpensive to hire a car and driver. Hire cars are especially useful if you want to explore the remoter reaches of Singapore, visit industrial areas, such as Jurong, or tour southern Malaysia. You will be charged an hourly rate and firms usually insist on a three-hour minimum charge. Even so, the cost is not much more than the equivalent taxi fare – depending, of course, on the type of car you hire. Reliable firms include **Elpin Tours and Limousines** (tel: 292 2388), **Presidential Pacific Limousine** (tel: 475 7833) and **Ways Plus Services** (tel: 338 8863).

Electricity

Singapore is on a 220–240 volt, 50 cycle system. Hotels are well used to supplying adaptors and transformers for visitors who need them.

Embassies

Australia: 25 Napier Road, tel: 737 9311.
Canada: 80 Anson Road, 14–00 IBM Towers, tel: 225 6363.
Ireland: 298 Tiong Bahru Road, 08–06 Tiong Bahru Plaza (tel: 276 8935).
UK (British): Tanglin Road, tel: 473 9333.
USA (American): 30 Hill Street, tel: 338 0251.

Emergency Telephone Numbers

Police	999
Ambulance	995
Fire	995

Entertainment

The *Straits Times* newspaper is the best place to look for listings and booking information. Many hotel travel desks will make bookings for you. There are booking agencies at Tangs department store and the Centrepoint Shopping Centre, both in Orchard Road.

Entry formalities see **Arriving**

Guidebooks

The Singapore Tourist Promotion Board publishes a good range of free information, which can be picked up from airport display stands on arrival, from hotels or from the Tourist Information offices in Raffles Hotel Arcade and Orchard Spring Lane Tourism Court (see **Tourist Offices** below for details of their opening times). Their publications include the *Singapore Official Guide* and the *Official Shopping Directory* published by CASE.

You will also find a plethora of free maps and shopping guides displayed in hotel foyers. Most of them are guaranteed to get you lost, confused or both. An exception is the clear and easily carried *Miller Freeman Map of Singapore*, which shows the locations of central hotels, shops, restaurants and tourist attractions. If you want a more comprehensive guide to eating out, look for *Singapore's 100 Best Restaurants*, compiled annually by the staff of *Tatler* magazine from readers' comments. If you want a pictorial souvenir, try the *Insight Guide: Singapore* (APA Publications) or *Singapore; State of the Art* (R Ian Lloyd Productions). Both are full of stunning pictures that will rekindle memories, interspersed with illuminating features on the history, people and culture of the island. **The Kinokuniya Bookshop** (Raffles City) and **MPH Bookstore** (Stamford Road) both keep a comprehensive stock of titles covering every aspect of Singapore.

Health
There are no special requirements for visitors (unless you are arriving from a cholera- or yellow fever-infected area – see page 107). Singapore is cleaner and healthier than many a Western city and even mosquitoes are no longer a problem, thanks to a successful campaign to eradicate the stagnant pools that form their breeding ground (mosquito cream is advisable if you plan to visit Malaysia, however). It is most unwise to expose yourself to the equatorial sun for very long or without a protective barrier. You will undoubtedly sweat if you walk very far so compensate for fluid loss by drinking fruit juices or water. Singapore's water is perfectly safe. Even so, you find that, in deference to Western qualms, water supplied in your hotel mini bar, and that used for ice cubes, will have been pre-boiled.

Fire walkers prepare for their ordeal at the Sri Mariamman Temple in Little India

Doctor/Dentist
Singapore's medical and dental facilities are among the best in the world. Overseas patients pay a slightly higher fee than locals. Visitors can also consult doctors at the following hospitals: Gleneagles Medical Centre (tel: 470 3415), Mount Alvernia Hospital (tel: 253 8023), Mount Elisabeth Hospital (tel: 737 2666), Singapore General Hospital (tel: 222 3322); or see the Singapore *Yellow Pages* under 'Dental Surgeons' and 'Medical Practitioners'.

Holidays
From a tourist point of view there is virtually no time when Singapore comes to a halt – shops are even open on Christmas Day. Chinese New Year is the big holiday, but even then you will find that it is business as usual amongst the large Indian and Malay communities. If you added together all the days that are special to Singaporean Christians, Muslims, Hindus and Chinese (see **Special Events** section) then nearly every day would be a holiday. As it is, the only official public holidays are:
New Year's Day (1 January)
Chinese New Year (2 days, late January or early February)
Good Friday
Hari Raya Puasa (dates follow the Islamic calendar)
Labour Day (1 May)
Vesak Day (mid-May)
Hari Raya Haji (one month after Hari Raya Puasa)
National Day (9 August)
Deepavali (late October or early November)
Christmas Day (25 December)

Lost Property
First check with the shop, restaurant, taxi firm or transport authority where the loss may have occurred – using the services of the hotel concierge, if necessary, to help you make the calls. If that fails, report your loss to the police. Singapore people are honest and will hand in property, so your chances of finding lost items are good. Don't forget, however, to report the loss of a passport to your embassy (see **Embassies** section) and to inform the relevant companies if you lose credit cards or travellers' cheques (see **Telephone** section for credit card company numbers).

Media
Local Newspapers The English-language *Straits Times*, founded in 1845, is still going strong and is regarded as Singapore's leading daily paper. Hotels often deliver complementary copies to your hotel room. The *Business Times*, as its name suggests, covers local company news. The *Straits Times* is well worth browsing through over breakfast, and not just for its entertainment columns; it will also give you an insight into Singaporean preoccupations – everything from the ponderous speeches of local politicians to the lifestyles of local yuppies and business tycoons.
Magazines and Foreign Media The *International Herald Tribune* is printed locally and available the same day. Overseas papers are generally on sale the day after publication in hotel news-stands and

Many of Chinatown's old shop-houses have been carefully renovated

bookshops such as **Kinokuniya** (Raffles City), **Times** (Centrepoint) and **MPH** (Stamford Road and Centrepoint). The same outlets stock a wide range of local and overseas magazines.

TV and Radio Check the *Straits Times* for details of programmes. Channel 5 broadcasts in English and Channel 8 in Mandarin, with English subtitles. Channel 12 broadcasts news, documentaries, sport and cultural programmes in English. BBC World Service broadcasts are relayed on 88.9Mhz. Otherwise take pot luck by tuning into Radio One (90.5Mhz) or Radio Ten (98.7Mhz) for an eclectic mix of talk, music and news; Radio Five (92.4Mhz) for serious music and classical, (95Mhz) for pop.

Money

Getting and using money in Singapore is easy if you are solvent. You can bring any amount in and you will have little difficulty in changing it into Singapore dollars, or any other currency, for that matter. If you plan lots of shopping, bring travellers' cheques or cash; you will get bigger discounts that way than paying by credit card.

Local Currency The Singapore dollar is strong and stable. Coins (issued in denominations of 1, 5, 10, 20, 50 and 100 cents) are essential for bus fares and MRT tickets – though there are machines in all MRT stations that will give you change for S$1 notes. Notes are issued in units of S$1 (being phased out), 2, 5, 10, 20, 50, 100, 500, 1,000 and 10,000. As in most parts of the world, you will not be much liked if you try to pay for taxis or small purchases with big notes; S$5, 10, 20 and 50 are the most useful ones to carry.

Do not accuse shopkeepers of ripping you off if they give you

Many temples are adorned with eye-catching roof carvings

Brunei notes in your change. Brunei dollars are completely interchangeable with Singaporean notes of the same value. Do not, however, accept Malaysian dollars (ringgit); they are not worth as much as Singaporean dollars and are no longer interchangeable.

Money Changers Singapore's money changers are an unusual phenomenon; they give better value than the banks, quite the reverse of one's expectations. Licensed money changers are ubiquitous; you will find them in every shopping centre (Change Alley, by the way, where you used to get the most competitive rates, is no more, swept away as part of a major redevelopment). Many of them double as tobacconists, newsagents or textile sellers, and most are open from 10.00 to 22.00hrs every day. It pays to shop around; rates from one dealer to another can vary by as much as 10 per cent, but all will give you a rate better than that of the banks for travellers' cheques and cash. It is always wise to confirm the rate, however, before you do a deal.

Banks Just about every international bank has a branch in Singapore and nearly all of them, local ones included, have a foreign exchange counter. They do not normally charge commission. Passports are required when you cash travellers' cheques or request a credit-card cash advance. For banking hours see **Opening times** below.

Credit Cards You should have no problem in paying for goods and services by credit card, though bear in mind that you will get bigger discounts in shops if you pay by cash or travellers' cheque. In the past, traders have tried to surcharge credit card users. This practice has now virtually stopped but if you are forced to pay a surcharge when purchasing goods by credit card, make sure that it is clearly shown as a separate item on your receipt. Forward this evidence to the card company and they will refund the charge, and deal with the offending shop.

Taxes The most important taxes you should be aware of are the 4 per cent room tax and 10 per cent service charge levied by all hotels. When you book a room, check whether the quoted price includes these charges – if not, don't forget to allow for an extra 14 per cent per room per day. As a rule hotels quote their prices net to make them look more competitive. If the hotel tariff has two 'plus' signs after the room rate (for example, S$150+ +) it means that tax and service are extra (so the true cost is S$170).

Opening Times

Government offices are usually open weekdays 08.00–17.00hrs and Saturdays 08.00–13.00hrs. Otherwise office hours vary from company to company. Singapore is a thriving capitalist enterprise and nobody thinks twice about working nights, weekends and holidays if there is money to be made. As a business visitor you will not find it difficult to make appointments for virtually any time of day. The same is true of stores – they are open just about every day of the year, though some up-market boutiques seem to think that the rich have an aversion to Sunday shopping and close on that day. Just about everyone else is open from 09.30 to 18.00hrs, and many shopping centres do not close until 21.00 or even 22.00hrs.

Bank hours are weekdays 10.00–15.00hrs (although some branches may open at 09.00hrs), Saturdays 09.30–13.00hrs (with some branches open until 15.00hrs), Sundays 09.30–15.00hrs (mostly branches in Orchard Road only).

For museum opening times, see individual entries in the **What to See** section.

Personal Safety

Singapore is a safe island and you need have no fear of attack when walking about the streets.

Pharmacies

Most shopping centres, department stores and supermarkets have a pharmacy and most are open from 09.00 to 22.00hrs. Many medicines are available without prescription and there will always be a qualified pharmacist on hand to give advice. Visitors with special drug needs will save the cost of a consultation if they bring an ample supply. Just in case, though, you should carry a letter from your practitioner detailing the medicines that have been prescribed.

Places of Worship

Temples

Visitors are welcome but etiquette must be observed. Shoes should be removed at mosques and Indian temples; Muslim mosques ask visitors not to wear shorts or backless/ sleeveless tops. Also, try to avoid interrupting worshippers. Most Indian places of worship are usually open until 20.00hrs.

Christian and Jewish Services

For times of services in English you can telephone the following establishments:

Anglican: St Andrew's Cathedral, Coleman Street, tel: 337 6104.

Baptist: International Baptist Church, 90 Kings Road, tel: 466 4911.

Methodist: Wesley Church, 5 Fort Canning Road, tel: 336 1433.

Roman Catholic: Cathedral of the Good Shepherd, Queen Street, tel: 337 2036.

Jewish: Jewish Synagogue, Waterloo Street, tel: 336 0692.

Police

In emergency, dial 999. Police posts are to be found at strategic points around Singapore. Those in tourist areas are well used to handling visitor enquiries and will do their best to help. Singapore's police try to maintain a balance between good community relations and crime prevention; they are fair but firm with offenders. If you break the law you can expect to be stopped and reminded of the rules, or issued with a fine ticket on the spot, depending on the severity of your offence. Equally you will find that Singapore people will not tolerate loutish behaviour and will ask you to desist – you will cause great offence, for example, if you drop litter (illegal) or jump queues (anti-social).
See also the section **Rules and Regulations**.

Post Office

Singapore's postal services are excellent. Post will normally reach its destination in five to 12 days – if not, the delay is usually caused at the receiving end. Most hotel reception desks or news-stands sell stamps for airmail letters and postcards, so you only need to visit a post office for registered and express mail or parcel services. Orchard Point Post Office, 160 Orchard Road (next to Centrepoint Shopping Centre), is the most convenient for most visitors and is open Monday to Saturday 08.30–18.00hrs. The Post Office at the Comcentre, 31 Exeter Road (near Somerset MRT station just off Orchard Road), has a 24-hour service for trunk calls and telegrams. Poste restante facilities are available at the General Post Office, Fullerton Building, Fullerton Road. This too has an annexe that never closes. Other post offices (over 60 in all) are generally open weekdays 09.00–17.00hrs; Saturdays 09.00–13.00hrs.

Public Transport

The centre of Singapore is compact and taxis are the best way of getting around. The Mass Rapid Transit system (known as the **MRT**) is very efficient but

When it starts to rain, jump in a taxi

you will often find that you still need a taxi to get from the station to your ultimate destination.

Taxis are plentiful at most times of the day or night, although you may have to wait between the peak hours of 07.30–09.00hrs and 16.30–18.00hrs on weekdays when everyone is trying to get to and from work, Saturday lunchtime when everyone is heading to or from the shops, and during heavy rainfall, when everyone who was planning to walk dives for the nearest taxi instead.

Five separate taxi firms operate in Singapore and you will soon come to recognise their distinctive vehicle liveries. Most cabs are clean, comfortable and air-conditioned. You can flag down a taxi anywhere, except where stopping restrictions apply, and there are ranks in main streets, near shopping centres and outside hotels. Hotel and restaurant staff will always call a cab for you if there is not one already waiting. If you are staying in the suburbs, visiting friends or on business, it is easy enough to telephone for a taxi. Your call will be answered in English. Tell them where you are and where you want to go. They will put out a radio message and confirm that a taxi will arrive 'in ten minutes' (they always say 'ten minutes', though the wait is often less). If they say 'no taxi', it simply means none of that company's taxis is in the vicinity. Try another number from the following:

CityCab, tel: 552 7200 or 552 7877;

Comfort Taxi Service, tel: 1800-452 5555;

Singapore Commuter, tel: 553 3488 (accepts Visa cards);

TIBS Taxis, tel: 481 1211;

Clementi Radio Taxis, tel: 467 2363.

All taxis have meters; if you intend to keep the cab for a long time, the driver will, however, usually negotiate an hourly rate. Downtown journeys rarely cost more than S$4 or $5 or so.

A table of extra charges is clearly displayed on passenger doors. These are not shown on the meter, so always ask the driver 'how much?'. Surcharges apply to journeys taken between midnight and 06.00hrs (50 per cent of the metered fare),

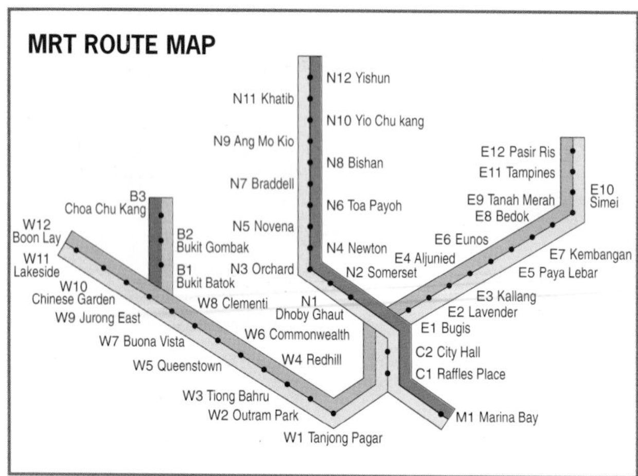

journeys starting at Changi Airport and journeys starting or ending in the Central Business District during peak hours. You also pay small extra charges for taxis booked by telephone and for baggage.

MRT (Metro) Singapore is rightly proud of its Mass Rapid Transit system (MRT), which moves commuters in and out of the centre swiftly and efficiently. It was designed to link the large suburban housing estates with the centre, so stations are not always located conveniently for tourist attractions. You will often have to complete your journey by bus or taxi. The MRT is, however, a good way of hopping around the Central Business District. Trains run at intervals of between three and eight minutes, depending on the time of day. The fares are very low and depend on the distance travelled. Clearly displayed signs explain the fare structure. Coin-operated ticket machines at the entrance to each station will give you change if you do not have the correct fare and there are machines that change S$1 notes. You can also buy stored-value cards.

Maps of the system are clearly displayed in stations and each line is colour-coded. All you have to do is decide which line to use, work out whether you are going north or south, east or west, and follow the signs.

Buses are efficient and inexpensive. If you intend to use them frequently it is worth buying a one-day or three-day Singapore Explorer ticket, giving unlimited travel by bus. These are cheap and come with a map of the system and a guide to which buses serve which tourist attractions. Explorer tickets can be bought at all hotels, from tour agents and from SBS (Singapore Bus Service) Travelcentres located at bus interchanges. If you do not have an Explorer ticket, you can buy the *Bus Guide* from newsagents for a few

cents. All bus stops are clearly marked and carry signboards listing nearby attractions. Fares depend on the distance travelled and you pay on entry; drivers will tell you what the fare is but they do not give change, so carry a supply of small coins.
Walking is essential for getting to know areas such as Chinatown or the colonial district but you are likely to perspire profusely if you try to tackle long distances without pauses for rest. Singapore does not tolerate jay walkers. It is illegal to cross roads near to a designated crossing, or to cross against a red light (see **Rules and Regulations** below). It is wise to obey this rule, if only because Singaporean drivers do not expect to encounter risk-taking pedestrians suddenly in their path.

Rules and Regulations
Singapore has a number of laws that visitors might consider an infringement upon their personal liberty. They have, however, made Singapore a pleasanter place and local people accept

The Mass Rapid Transit system is easy to use, with colour-coded routes across the city

them in that spirit. If you infringe the rules, do not be surprised if a passer-by stops and reminds you of the laws; they are being helpful, rather than officious, and are simply concerned to prevent you from being fined.

Smoking is forbidden in all restaurants and air-conditioned shopping centres, in taxis, buses and the MRT, in lifts, theatres and cinemas and in Government offices. Many non-Government offices have imposed their own smoking ban.

Chewing Gum, this is now illegal and the sale of gum is banned.

Littering of any kind is subject to a hefty fine. This law, backed by an army of street cleaners, is one reason why Singapore is such a pleasant environment to be in.

Jaywalking According to the law you can be fined for crossing a red pedestrian light or crossing a road within 50 metres of an underpass, pedestrian bridge or designated crossing.

Drugs Very severe penalties await anyone foolish enough to get involved with narcotics. The mere possession of cannabis can result in a 10-year prison sentence, and the death sentence is mandatory for anyone found guilty of trafficking in heroin or morphine – remember even possession can be viewed as 'trafficking'.

Telephones

Out and about in Singapore you will find payphones everywhere – either Telecom street booths or bright orange telephones in shops, restaurants and hotel lobbies. Local calls cost 10 cents for three minutes, with a maximum duration of nine minutes – after that you will be cut off automatically. Many Telecom booths accept phone cards that can be purchased at Post Offices, newsagents and hotel reception desks, denominated in values of S$2, S$5, S$10, $20 and $50. They can be used for both local and overseas calls.

Virtually all hotels provide International Direct Dial (IDD) telephones in their rooms but, in common with practice the world over, they will charge you a substantial premium for their use. It is cheaper to make international calls from the Telecom phonebooths that you will find near or in any central shopping centre. You can also make international calls, and send faxes, from the GPO Fullerton Building, Fullerton Road (the annexe is open 24 hours) or the Comcentre, 31 Exeter Road (24hrs – trunk calls, telegrams).

To call another country from Singapore dial 001, followed by the country code, the town code (minus the initial 0) and the subscriber's number.

To call Singapore from another country dial the IDD access code (00 in the UK, 011 in the US), followed by 65 then the subscriber's number.

For local Directory Enquiries in Singapore dial 100. For help in making overseas calls (including collect calls and charge-card calls) dial 104 – except for Malaysia, in which case dial 109.

Some useful numbers:

Police emergency 999

Ambulance and fire 995

Tourist information 1800–334 1335/6, 1800–738 3778

Touristline (24-hr automated enquiry system) 1800–831 3311

Taxi services 1800–452 5555, 1800–552 2600
AA Road Service (24-hour) 748 9911
Speaking clock 1711
Singapore Bus Service 287 2727
Flight information 1800–542 4422
Rail enquiries 222 5165
Immigration department 532 2877
Embassies: Australia 737 9311; Canada 225 6363; Ireland 733 2180; New Zealand 235 9966; UK 473 9333; US 338 0251.
Consumer complaints: Singapore Tourist Promotion Board 736 6622; Consumers' Association 270 4611.
Credit card companies: American Express 1800–732 2244; Diners 294 4222; MasterCard 533 2888; Visa 1800-345 1345.

Temples see **Places of Worship**

Time
Singapore is eight hours ahead of London GMT, 15 hours ahead of Los Angeles, 13 hours ahead of New York, 2 hours behind Sydney, 4 hours behind Auckland.

Tipping
This practice is discouraged by the Government but, human nature being what it is, many service providers still expect it. A service charge is automatically added to hotel bills but porters and room service waiters will still linger hoping for a dollar or two. Central restaurants usually levy a service charge too, though out of town restaurants tend to leave it to your discretion. There is no need to tip at hawker food stalls. Tipping is prohibited at the airport.

Toilets
The easiest toilets to locate are those in hotel lobbies, though shopping centres have them too, as do cinemas, theatres, restaurants, museums and tourist venues. Most are impeccably clean since failure to flush toilets and urinals will result in a stiff reprimand from the attendant.

Singapore is a young nation

Most Singaporeans are Chinese and the influence of their culture can be seen in many stunning buildings

Tourist Offices

In Singapore Ground floor, Tourism Court, 1 Orchard Spring Lane, tel: 1–800–738 3778/ 738 3779. *Open*: daily, 08.30–18.00; 328 North Bridge Road, 02–34 Raffles Hotel Arcade, tel: 1–800–334 1335/334 1336. *Open*: daily, 08.30–20.00hrs.

Overseas Australia: Singapore Tourist Promotion Board (STPB), Suite 1202, Level 12, Westpac Plaza, 60 Margaret Street, Sydney, NSW 2000, tel: 02-241 3771/2; STPB, 8th Floor St Georges Court, 16 St Georges Terrace, Perth, WA 6000, tel: 09-325 8578.

Canada: Standard Life Centre, 121 King Street West, Suite 1000, Toronto, Ontario, M5H 3T9, tel: 416/363 8898.

New Zealand: 3rd floor, 43 High Street, Auckland, tel: (09) 358 1191.

UK: STPB, 1st Floor, Carrington House, 126–130 Regent Street, London W1R 5FE, tel: 0171 437 0033.

US: STPB, 590 Fifth Avenue, 12th Floor, New York, NY 10036, tel: 212/302 4861; STPB, 8484 Wilshire Boulevard, Suite 510, Beverly Hills, Los Angeles CA 90211, tel: 213/852 1901; STPB,

Two Presidential Plaza, 180N Stetson Avenue, Suite 1450, Chicago, Illinois 60601, tel: 312/938 1888.

Tour Operators
Visitors tend to visit Singapore for two or three days and try to fit as much as possible into their short stay. Knowing this, tour operators have packaged Singapore into manageable bites – most tours last around three hours with departures typically at 09.00 and 14.00hrs.
Tours and operators are vetted by the Singapore Tourist Promotion Board, so the standard is high. There are some 37 different options, ranging from a basic familiarisation trip to harbour cruises, World War II battlefield tours, Round-the-Island tours and even tea at the Zoo with the chimpanzees. Costs are very reasonable and every hotel has a tour desk where you can obtain full details and arrange for bookings to be made.

Discover Singapore on the Net
Potential visitors to Singapore can now browse the Internet to uncover the city's attractions. Launched in 1995, the Singapore Online Guide (SOG) features tourist attractions, hotels and room rates, transportation, maps of Singapore and business information. There is also an 'interactive travel agent' which allows you to key in your interests and recieve a travel package tailored to individual needs. The SOG (which will be updated on a regular basis) is located at:
http://www.travel.com.sg on the World Wide Web platform.

Inevitably these tours are designed for Mr and Mrs Average. If you want something tailored to your personal interests, contact the Registered Tourist Guides Association (tel: 339 2110 or 339 2113). The cost of a personal guide is again very reasonable – about S$18 for an English-speaking guide for half a day. All registered guides receive a thorough training and you can usually request a guide with specialist knowledge – whether it be architecture, wildlife or simply the best places to shop.

Travel Agencies
There are more than 300 registered travel agents in Singapore so competition is fierce and it is well worth comparing prices. All agencies are licensed by the government and their standards monitored, so contact the Singapore Tourist Promotion Board if you have a complaint (tel: 736 6622). You will find a complete listing in the Singapore *Yellow Pages*, but usually you will not have to look further than your hotel reception desk or shopping arcade.

LANGUAGE
Singapore has four official languages (English, Malay, Mandarin and Tamil), as well as an unofficial one – Singlish, a blend of English, Chinese and Malay. In practice it is English that binds this multi-ethnic state, and it is rare to find anyone under 45 years of age who does not speak it well. Even the older generation speaks it, but often with the intonation of mother tongue, so you may have to listen hard to understand.

INDEX

Page numbers in *italics* refer to illustrations.

Abu Bakar Mosque 38–9
accommodation 77–84, 97
agriculture 54
airport and air services 107-8
airport taxes 108
Arab Street 17, 20, 76
Armenian Apostolic Church of St Gregory 20
Asian Village 44

baby-sitting services, 97, 108
banks 116–17
bargaining 70–1
Batam 17, 35
belukar woodland 54
Bintan 17, 35
Bird Concert 20, *20*
birdlife 50, 51, 52, 53, *53*
Boat Quay 25
Botanic Gardens 21, 49
breakdowns 112
budget tips 97
Bukit Timah 21, 49
Bukit Timah Nature Reserve 21–2, 52, *54*
bumboat cruises 33, 34
buses 120–1
Butterfly Park 44

cabaret 90
camping 108
Cantonese cuisine 59–60
car rental 111
Cavenagh Footbridge 30
Cenotaph 30
Central Business District *5–6*, 111
Changi Airport 76, 107–8, *109*
Changi Prison Chapel and Museum 22
chauffeur-driven cars 112
Chettiar Temple 22
children's entertainment 96–7
Chinaman Scholars Gallery 22
Chinatown *23*, 23–5, *71*, *76*
Chinese and Japanese Gardens 26, *26*
Chinese New Year 98–9
Chingay 99
Christmas in Singapore 103
cinema 85–6
City Hall 29
Clarke Quay 25
classical concerts 86
climate and seasons 49, 91
coach services 108
colonial Singapore 27–30
complaints system 109
Conrad, Joseph 10
coral reefs 52
counterfeit goods 69
credit cards 71, 117
cricket 28, 104
crime 109
Crocodile Farms 31, *31*
cultural events 86, 87–9
currency 115–6
customs regulations 110–11

Deepavali 103
delivery and shipping of goods 72
department stores 72
disabled travellers 111
discos 86–7
Dragon Boat Festival 100–1
dress 91
drinking water 113
driving 111–12
drug offences 122
duty-free allowances 110

economic growth 12–13
embassies 112
emergencies 112
Empress Place Building 31
entertainment and nightlife 85–90, 112
entry formalities 107

ferries 35
Festival of the Hungry Ghosts 101–2
Festival of the Nine Emperor Gods 103
festivals and events 98–103, *101*
food and drink 55–68
football 104
Fort Canning 32
Fort Canning Aquarium 47
Fort Siloso 44
Fuk Tak Chi Temple 32
Fullerton Building 30

gardens 21, 26
General Post Office 30
golf 104–5
Good Retailers Scheme 70
guidebooks 111, 112–13
Guinness World of Records 32

Hajjah Fatimah Mosque 20
Harbour and River Cruises 33–4
harbour 33, *33*
Hari Raya Haji 101
Hari Raya Puasa 100
Haw Par Villa 34, *34*, *96*
hawker food stalls 68, *92*
health matters 107, 113–14
history of Singapore 9–12
Hokkien cuisine 61
Holland Village 76
horse racing 104
hotels 78–84
hostels 84

Indian cuisine 65
Indonesia 35

islands 35–6
Istana Besar 39

Japanese cuisine 66
jaywalking 121, 122
Johor Bahru 38–9
Jurong 17
Jurong Bird Park 36, *36, 51*
Jurong Crocodile Paradise 31

Kampong Glam 20
karaoke bars 89
Kranji 52
Kranji War Memorial 36
Kusu 35–6
Kusu Pilgrimage 103

Labrador Nature Reserve Park 49
language 92–3, 125
Lim Bo Seng Memorial 30
litter fines 122
Little India 37, 76
local customs 93–4
local etiquette 94–5, 121
local time 123
lost property 114

Malacca *38–9*, 39
Malay/Indonesian cuisine 58–9
Malaysia 38–9
Mandai Orchid Gardens 39, *39*
mangroves 50–2
maps
Chinatown 24
colonial Singapore & Fort Canning 28–9
islands 35
MRT (metro) 120
Orchard Road 74–5
Sentosa 44
Singapore 14–15
Singapore city 18–19
Southeast Asia 4
Maritime Museum 44
Maugham, Somerset 10
media 114–15
medical treatment 113–14
Merlion Park, *7, 27*, 30
money 115–17
money changers 116
Monkey God Feast 100
Mooncake Festival 102, *102*
mosques 20, 38–9
MRT (metro) 120, *121*
museums 22, 31, 41–2, 44–45

National Art Gallery *40*, 41
National Day 102
National Museum 41
National Orchid Garden 21, *21*
nature reserves 21–2, 36, 49
Navarathri (Nine Nights) Festival 102–3
newspapers and magazines 114–15
Nogore Durgha shrine 25
Nonya cuisine 56, 58
North Boat Quay 30

opening hours 71, 117
opera 88, *88*
Orchard Road 72–5, *73*
orchids 20, 21 39, *39*

Padang 27, 28
parking 111–12
Parkway Parade 76
Parliament House 29–30
passports and visas 107
Peking cuisine 61–2
Peranakan Place Museum 41–2
personal safety 117
pharmacies 117–18
Pioneers of Singapore 43–4
places of worship 118
police 118
polo 104, *104–5*
Ponggal 98
population diversity 92
post offices 118
prohibited goods 71, 110
public holidays 114
public transport 118–21
pubs and bars 89–90

Qing Ming 100
Queen Elizabeth Walk 30

radio and television 115
Raffles, Sir Stamford 7, 8, 9, 21, 30, 32
Raffles Hotel *8–9*, 42
rail travel 108
rainforests 52–4
Ramadan 100
Rare Stone Museum 44
reservoir parks 49, 52
restaurants 55
  Cantonese 59–60
  Hokkien 61
  Indian 65
  Japanese 66
  Malay/Indonesian 58–9
  Nonya 56, *57*, 58
  Peking 61–2
  seafood 62–4
  Szechuan 62
  Thai 66
  Western 66–7
Ridley, Henry 20, 21
river cruises 33–4
rugby 104
rules and regulations 13, 121–2

sailing 105
St Andrew's Cathedral 27
St John's 35–6
Sakya Muni Temple 42, *42*
seafood 62–5
Seletar estuary 49, 52
Sentosa Island *43*, 43–4
Serangoon estuary 50–52
Serangoon Road 37
shopping 69–76
shopping guides, 72, 112–13
Singapore Cricket Club 28, *28*
Singapore Crocodilarium 31

Singapore Recreation Club 29
Singapore River 17
Singapore Science Centre 45, *45*
'Singapore Sling' 42
Siong Lim Temple *16*, 45
smoking bans 122
songbirds *10*, 20
speed limits 111
sport and leisure activities 104–5
Sri Mariamman Temple 46, *46–7*
Sultan Mosque 20
Sungei Buloh 50
Supreme Court 29
Surrender Chamber 43–4
swimming pools 97
Szechuan cuisine 62

tailoring 71–2
Tanjong Pager Restoration Area 25
Tanjung Pinang 35
taxes
airport 108
hotel 117
on purchases 69
taxis 119–20
tea-dances 96
telephones 122–3
Temple of the Calm Sea 25
Temple of a Thousand Lights 42, *42*
temples 22, 25, 32, 35, 42, 45, 46–7, 118
Thai cuisine 66
Thaipusam 98
Thian Hock Keng Temple 46–7
Thimithi 103
tipping 123
toilets 123
tour operators 125
tourist offices 124–5
travel agencies 125
Tua Pek Kong temple 35

Underwater World 44

vaccinations 107
Vesak Day 100
Victoria Memorial Hall 30
Victoria Theatre 30
voltage 112

Wak Hai Cheng Bio 25
walking in Singapore 121–2
War Memorial Park 30
watersports 105
Western cuisine 66–7
Wildlife and countryside 49–54

yacht charter 34
YMCA 84, 97
youth hostel 97

Zoological Gardens 48, *48*

Acknowledgements

The Automobile Association would like to thank the following photographers, libraries and associations for their assistance in the preparation of this book.

PAUL KENWARD took all the photographs in this book (© AA PHOTO LIBRARY) except:
AA PHOTO LIBRARY 23, 28, 119 (A Kouprianoff) and 8/9, 54 (K Paterson).
NATURE PHOTOGRAPHERS LTD 50/1 Jurong Bird Garden (S C Bisserott), 52/3 Brahminy Kite (K J Carlson)
PICTURES COLOUR LIBRARY Cover Chinese Dragon.
SINGAPORE PROMOTIONS & P R DEPARTMENT 5/6 Singapore skyline, 45 Science Centre, 55 Satay, 57 Cakes.
SPECTRUM COLOUR LIBRARY 7 Merlion Park, 13 Lady in costume, 16 Siong Lim Temple, 38/9 Malacca waterfront, 42 Sakya Muni Temple, 46/7 Sri Mariamman Temple, 73 Orchard Road, 85 Dragon dance, 116 Buddhist Temple.

Thanks also to the **Automobile Association of Singapore** for their assistance in updating the Directory section for this revised edition.